THE FITNESS BOOK

Jane Hyman, M.Ed.
Barbara Millen Posner, D.P.H., R.D.

Julian Messner New York

Published by Julian Messner,
A Division of Simon & Schuster, Inc.
Simon & Schuster Building,
1230 Avenue of the Americas,
New York, New York 10020.
Also available in a Wanderer hardcover edition.
JULIAN MESSNER and colophon are trademarks of
Simon & Schuster, Inc.

Manufactured in the United States of America

Designed by Stanley S. Drate

10 9 8 7 6 5 4 3 2 1

Library of Congress Cataloging in Publication Data

Hyman, Jane.
  The Fitness book.

  Bibliography: p.
  Includes index.
  Summary: A handbook discussing personal diet and fitness
goals, with practical advice on how to achieve them.
  1. Reducing diets—Juvenile literature. 2. Reducing
exercises—Juvenile literature. 3. Youth—Nutrition—
Juvenile literature. 4. Exercise for children—Juvenile
literature. [1. Nutrition. 2. Exercise. 3. Weight
control] I. Posner, Barbara Millen. II. Title.
III. Series.
RM222.2.H96   1984   613.2′5′088055   83-23392
ISBN 0-671-46433-7 (pbk.)
ISBN 0-671-46741-7 (lib. bdg.)

Authors and publisher would like to thank the following for permission to reproduce their materials:

On pp. 18-19, the physical growth record charts are reprinted by permission of the American Medical Association.

On pp. 23-24, the average heights and weights and recommended energy intake chart and recommended vitamin and mineral intake chart are adapted from *Recommended Dietary Allowances,* National Academy Press, Washington, D.C., 1980.

On pp. 68-73, the exchange lists (Trade Units) from the American Diabetes Association, Inc., and the American Dietetic Association, from the EXCHANGE LISTS FOR MEAL PLANNING which were prepared by committees of the American Diabetes Association, Inc., and The American Dietetic Association in cooperation with the National Institute of Arthritis, Metabolism and Digestive Diseases and the National Heart and Lung Institute, National Institutes of Health, Public Health Service, U.S. Department of Health, Education and Welfare.

On pp. 78-80, the procedure for estimating body fat from Gaillard, B., Haskell, W., Smith, N. and Ogilvie, B.: *Handbook for the Young Athelete,* p. 22 Bull Publishing Company, 1978. P.O. Box 208; Palo Alto, California 94302.

On p. 81, the heart rate chart from *Practical Measurements for Evaluation in Physical Education,* 3rd ed., by Barry L. Johnson and Jack K. Nelson. Reprinted by permission of the author, Dr. Barry L. Johnson.

DEDICATION

For my parents, Irene and Kermit Robinson; two special dieters, Lauri and Carole; and a wonderful friend and editor, Wendy Barish

For Marshall and Bowen for their patience, enthusiasm, and constant flow of energy and my parents, Grace Theilacker Millen and F. J. Millen, M.D.

ACKNOWLEDGMENTS

It is with great sincerity that we express our appreciation to Connie Dillner Roberts, M.S., R.D., Coordinator of the Nutrition Consultation Service, Sharon D. Jackson, M.S., R.D., Nutritionist at the Brigham and Women's Hospital, Boston, Claire Regan, M.S., R.D., and Marlene O'Donnell, M.S., R.D. All provided extensive background information for this project from their research in and personal experiences with adolescent and adult weight loss and nutrition. In addition, we are grateful to Dr. Beverly Bullen, Director of the Graduate Nutrition Program at Boston University, for providing helpful comments and the nutritional implications of exercise and to Gretchen M. von Meering, B.S., Fitness Director of the Skyclub Executive Fitness Center, Boston.

CONTENTS

1

So You Think You Know Yourself?

You're a teenager, or perhaps just about to enter your teens. This is a very special time in your life, a time when your body is changing very quickly, when you care very much what other people and friends think about you, and a time when you think a lot about yourself.

Adolescence: A Time of Conflict

Have you suddenly seemed to grow tall? Or to gain weight? These physical changes are part of the normal growth spurts for teens, but they may make you feel strange and alien toward your own body. Maybe you feel too large or awkward. Perhaps one part of your body seems too small and another part seems too large. Sometimes your arms and legs grow larger before the rest of you fills out. Your balance may be off and you may feel unsure about what to do with your longer body parts. This is normal; it's also normal for you to spend a lot of time looking at yourself in a mirror.

Remember that growth rates are individualized. Each person grows at a different age and at different speeds. This may be hard for you to accept, since most teenagers prefer to be just like one another. If you mature later than others, some friends may still think of you as a child. If you mature early, some friends may expect you to act older than you really are. Between the ages of ten and thirteen girls usually are taller than boys. Boys often begin their growth spurts two years later when they're between twelve and fifteen. As a teen, you care a lot about what other people think of you. Beware of the "perfect" teenager you see in magazines, on television, and in the movies—he or she rarely exists. Feel good about yourself. You are special!

Do Teens Diet?

If you think that a fairly large number of your class-mates go on some kind of diet, you're right! The name or type of diet may change, just as fads change, but for many teens, as well as adults, dieting seems to be the usual condition rather than just an occasional thing.

Most teens would rather lose weight by dieting than by changing their exercise habits. For every three girls who go on a diet, there is only one girl who tries to change her weight by getting more exercise. For every two boys who choose to exercise to lose weight, three boys choose to diet instead. In a typical senior high class, 15 out of 100 girls and 5 out of 100 boys are dieting.

Diet Abuse

In our culture being slim is in. Some teenagers begin to feel that they must stay thin at any cost. This attitude is the reason so many new fad diets become so popular. Diets that push a single food item such as grapefruit ultimately lead to problems. Many people who go on these diets think the food works like magic. They don't take on the real challenge of weight loss themselves, and such unbalanced diets can be dangerous and result in malnutrition. Beware! The signs of malnutrition may be hard for you to see. You could be tired or just have a change in your feelings. *But most important of all, fad diets will not teach you eating habits that will help you to maintain your weight loss permanently.* If you lose weight on a fad diet, as soon as you go off the diet you'll probably regain the weight you lost—and then feel as if you've failed!

Have you heard the words "anorexia nervosa," "bulimarexia" or "bulimia"? These are medical terms used to describe conditions that are very serious and may be life threatening.

Anorexia nervosa is a form of self-starvation. The anorexic suffers from a deep-rooted fear of gaining weight and a mixed-up image of the body. This person, usually a girl, does not believe her body is very thin even if it is. The most obvious symptom is extreme weight loss, at least 25 percent of the original body weight, while on a strict diet. About half of the anorectics go on eating binges followed by self-induced vomiting. They may also rely on diet pills and laxatives to keep their weight down. Although it's hard to get exact statistics because many with this problem do not seek medical help, it is estimated that there are 50 to 75 cases of anorexia nervosa per 100,000 people, with a mortality (death) rate of 10 to 15 percent.

Bulimarexia or bulimia is another eating disorder. Bulemics fear weight gain just as anorectics do. Victims of bulimarexia may eat up to 55,000 calories in an hour or two and then start vomiting. This binge-purge pattern may be repeated as often as four times a day. Sometimes bulemics take laxatives, as many as 300 a week, to stop their bodies from gaining weight. The bulemic is usually at or near normal weight. The eating-purging behavior is done in private so others often don't know what's happening.

If you know anyone who may have a serious eating disorder you may want to call or write the Anorexia Nervosa and Associated Disorders Organization (ANAD), a national nonprofit group that helps victims and their families.

ANAD
Suite 2020
550 Frontage Road
Northfield, Illinois 60093
hotline: (312) 831-3438

When Not to Diet

If you were to restrict your caloric intake during the year of your maximum growth spurt, it's highly likely you could end up reducing your chances to reach your maximum height. Height growth can be stunted if you rob your body of the calories and nutrients it needs in order to allow such things as bones and skin to grow.

Be sure to check the growth charts to see where you are in terms of your own growth spurt. Growth spurts occur at different ages for boys and girls. Also, the spurt is different from person to person. Don't be alarmed if you start growing faster than some of your classmates. Don't push a panic button if your friends seem to be growing before your eyes. In general, you will probably sprout up in the two years before puberty. These years before puberty are called the maximum growth age. Puberty marks the peak of the growth rate curve.

So what's puberty? Puberty is the time in your life at which sexual maturity begins. For girls, puberty starts with the first menstrual flow, even though it may be skimpy or irregular. For boys, there are a number of signs. The most reliable one is probably the presence of spermatozoa (sperm) in the urine, which can be seen under the microscope. On the surface of the body the development of the secondary sex characteristics express changes that are happening inside the body. Both girls and boys develop pubic and armpit hair. Facial hair for boys may come first. Chest hair generally appears only late in the teens. A common age for the start of puberty for girls is twelve, although it ranges from ten to fifteen years of age. For boys, a common age for the start of puberty is fourteen, although the range can be from twelve to seventeen years of age.

For all these changes to occur, the body needs to receive enough energy and other nutrients from food. That's why dieting using a low-calorie weight-reduction program is usually not recommended in early pre-puberty ages.

Another time not to diet is during teenaged pregnancy. If a teen fails to increase her food intake or loses weight, both she and her baby face health risks. A pregnant teenager needs to be under the direct supervision of a doctor. The physician or professional registered nutritionist will guide the pregnant teen's diet.

Here is one last and very important piece of advice: *Don't diet if you're not ready or don't want to diet!* If you diet just because your parents, a relative, or maybe a friend wants you to diet, or dares you to, you probably won't be successful. Diet because you know the time is right and *you* want to do it!

When Is It Safe to Diet?

A diet for weight reduction can be safe once you have passed the maximum growth spurt. Remember, to grow properly, your body needs the right nutrients. A low-calorie diet, even one supplemented with vitamins, can't give you all you need. Moderate weight-loss rates are strongly recommended. A diet should be about 1200 calories or more a day and include some physical activity. A one- to two-pound weight loss per week is thought best.

It is safe for you to go on an unsupervised diet if you do not have diabetes, have no other health or emotional problems, are not pregnant, and are not recovering from an illness. If you want to lose more than ten pounds, it's recommended that you speak to a doctor for a medically supervised program.

Dieting "Booby Traps"

Your goal is to succeed. You need to be your own "coach." One thing a good coach does is prepare the team for any invisible obstacles. The coach wants the team to win. Part of the winning strategy is to recognize and plan for the management of hurdles. To approach weight control without strategies to deal with obstacles is like playing soccer or field hockey without the protective gear. You increase the risk of getting hurt and dropping out of the game.

Your family may be your first booby trap. Have you heard that obesity runs in families? Statistics do tell us that if neither parent is fat, there's only a 7 percent chance that their child will be fat. If one parent is obese, the chance jumps up to 40 percent, and if both parents are obese, the chance that their child will be obese increases to 80 percent. This suggests that there may be some hereditary link to obesity, but you need not feel doomed. It's very rare that the cause of overweight is a glandular or metabolic problem. It's true that you may have to work harder to combat the statistics, but it doesn't automatically lead to obesity. It's only an inherited *potential,* not a sure-fire outcome. You have the ability to overcome a family tendency for being overweight by controlling what you eat.

Another strong family booby trap is food patterns. You may be overweight because your parents taught you their poor eating habits. You may have been encouraged to overeat. Did someone ever say to you: "Clean your plate," "Eat for the starving children," "Stop crying and I'll give you candy"? Food may have been used as a reward for being good or withheld as a form of punishment. In addition, almost every ethnic group has traditional fattening foods, such as potatoes and gravy, sour cream and blintzes, greens with bacon fat, fried beans, antipasto. You may now be at a stage in growing up when it's time to strike out on your own and develop healthful eating patterns.

Our society has also made it difficult to remain on a healthful diet. Food manufacturers spend a 1.2 billion dollar budget annually on food advertising. The food industry has learned to package its products to attract consumers. Some foods look very appealing and are hard to resist. Our environment is filled with food, food that is already processed and ready to eat. You need only take off the wrapper.

Friends may also be a booby trap. You're often in a rush when you do things together, grabbing food on the run from what is available. Or your friends may tease you if you buy milk from a vending machine instead of a Coke or Pepsi. You will need to have confidence to make the decisions that are best for you.

You may be your own worst enemy. Are you too hard on yourself? Are you harder on yourself than you are on your friends? You don't have to be successful one hundred percent of the time. Remember, a cupcake *can* be worked in and still keep the day's calories under the limit necessary for weight control. The smart teen is one who plans to save a few calories by sometimes omitting a slice of bread and butter in order to have and enjoy a cupcake without guilt. Set realistic expectations for yourself and you will succeed.

2

Facts You Need to Know

You're probably reading this book because you've decided to go on a diet. Maybe all your friends are dieting and you want to do what they do. If the time is right for you, then before you begin your diet, you need to know some important facts. What is your ideal weight? How do you diet and still meet your body's energy and nutrient requirements? In other words, what are your goals and how do you reach them safely?

Throughout this book you'll be asking yourself many questions. You'll also be making plans and keeping track of your progress. To help you organize this information, you might want to get a notebook or make a scrapbook for your personal dieting log.

Desirable Weights

How much should you weigh? To answer that question you must know something about how you're growing. The charts in this chapter will help you figure that out.

15

The numbers on these physical growth charts come from scientific studies of many boys and girls as they grew from ages four to eighteen.

Find the chart for your sex. As you look at the charts you can see:

1. Ages are shown along the bottom and in the middle in yearly spaces.
2. Height is marked along the upper right and left sides of the chart in inches and centimeters.
3. Weight is listed along the lower right and left sides of the chart in units of pounds and kilograms.
4. There are three areas or zones for heights and three zones for weights. Be sure to note that each weight zone goes with a matching shade in a height zone. For example, "above average" in the weight zone matches "tall" in the height zone. The zones of weight are wider than the zones for height. That's because boys and girls of the same age *normally* are more different in weight than in height.

To find your growth pattern, follow these steps:

STEP 1: Find your height along the left side.
STEP 2: Find your age in the middle of the chart.
STEP 3: Follow these numbers toward the center until they meet.
STEP 4: This meeting point is your *height zone*.
STEP 5: Using the lower half of the chart, find your *weight zone* in the same way.
STEP 6: Put the date and your height and weight zones on a piece of paper or in a notebook.

Write down your height and weight every six months. You may change zones during your growth periods. For example, when you were ten or eleven years old you may have been in the "average" zones for both height and weight. Now you may be in the "tall" and "above average" zones. This may be your growth pattern.

Look carefully at the zones you're in for both height and weight. If your height and weight are in matching zones, you're probably growing evenly. You're in good proportion. All three zones are normal. But remember, you needn't feel that you should be in the "average" zone!

Be careful not to confuse "above average" with "fat." For example, a tall athlete whose weight is above average is likely to be very lean and yet weigh more than average. Don't let words mislead you.

One final note of caution. It's important to realize that you'll grow much more quickly when you're an adolescent than you did when you were a child. You may even have different growth rates during different periods of your adolescent years. Try to keep your height and weight in matching zones. Keep track of your progress.

To define your ideal body weight, locate a weight range in the same zone as your height. For example, a girl who is five feet four inches tall and sixteen years old may weigh from 115 to 135 pounds and still be considered in an appropriate weight zone. A weight below this would be considered below the average zone and may not be healthy for a given individual.

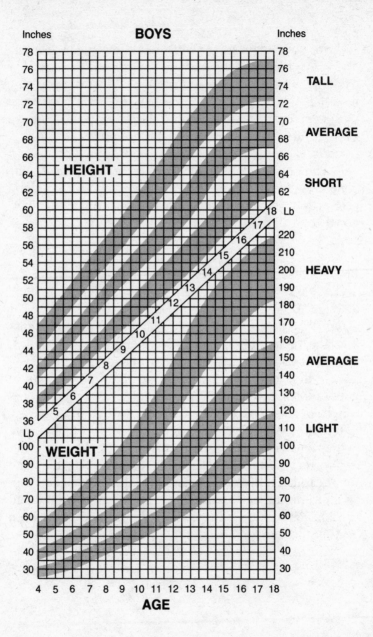

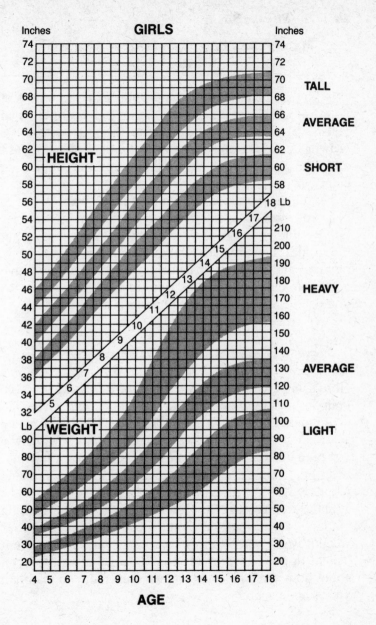

GIRLS

Maintaining Energy and General Nutrient Requirements

If you're an adolescent, then you can see how fast your body is changing. This is the time in your life when you have many nutrient requirements because you are growing and developing new body tissue. The amount of exercise you do each day will change the amount of calories you need to grow properly.

There's a quick rule of thumb you may want to use to help you make a good guess about how many calories you would need to take in each day to keep your weight the same. For females, take your current weight in pounds, and multiply that weight by 17. This will give you your maintenance calories, or how many calories you need each day to maintain your same weight.

FEMALES:
current weight (lbs) × 17 = maintenance calories

Here's an example. If a female currently weighs 100 pounds, multiply 100 times 17, which would give 1700 maintenance calories (100 × 17 = 1700 maintenance calories). This means that for a female who now weighs 100 pounds, she may eat about 1700 calories a day and keep her weight the same, assuming she is exercising moderately.

Males can also use this quick rule of thumb for figuring out maintenance calories, but instead of multiplying your weight by 17, you multiply by 20. You take your current weight in pounds, multiply by 20, and that will tell you about how many calories you need each day to maintain your same weight.

MALES:
current weight (lbs) × 20 = maintenance calories

If you want to lose weight, then you might need to eat fewer calories than the maintenance calorie amount you just figured out. But your body is growing and you do need a certain number of calories each day to make sure your body gets the energy it needs to help it grow.

The energy charts in this chapter will help you figure out how many calories your growing body needs. The energy values are given by sex, age, height, and weight. The calorie amounts listed are average daily energy requirements. These amounts assume that you will only be doing light exercise. If you exercise more, you will probably need to take in more calories or you might not get enough essential nutrients.

Protein is one of those important nutrients that help your body develop new tissue. If over long periods of time you don't take in enough calories, then your body will begin to use its stores of protein, a condition one should avoid.

Here's a quick way to figure out your protein needs. First take your body weight in pounds and multiply that number by 0.36. This will give you a good estimate of how many *grams* of protein you need each day.

Body Weight (lbs) × 0.36 = estimated grams of protein
needed each day

To convert the grams to ounces, take the gram amount you just arrived at, and divide it by 7. This will give you a good estimate of the number of ounces of high quality protein you need each day.

Grams ÷ 7 = approximate ounces of high quality
protein needed each day

Here's an example. If a male weights 120 pounds, he
would multiply 120 by 0.36 and get 43.2 grams of protein
needed each day (120 × 0.36 = 43.2). Then, to convert
the grams to ounces, he would take 43.2 and divide it by
7 to get approximately 6 ounces of high quality protein
needed each day (43.2 ÷ 7 = approximately 6). You can
get high quality protein most easily from lean meat, fish,
poultry, cheese, milk and many vegetarian dishes.

Your body needs other nutrients besides protein to
help it grow. The National Research Council has provided recommended levels of many major nutrients
needed during adolescence. You'll find this information
on the vitamin and mineral charts in this chapter. In the
appendix you'll find charts that list foods you can eat to
help you get enough of each vitamin and mineral. You'll
also find a listing of the vitamins and minerals found in
your favorite foods and in fast foods in other charts in the
appendix.

The best way to be sure that all these requirements are
met is to eat a balanced and mixed diet. If you're growing
normally, that's a good sign that your needs are being
met.

Are you confused? Did you realize that your body
needed so many different things? Why do you need all
those nutrients?

Here are just a few of the known major roles of some
key nutrients. Vitamin A is important for seeing well in
dim light; it also helps you grow and helps to maintain the
skin and the tissue in your intestines. Vitamin D is
needed for bone growth and development. Vitamin E

helps to keep your cells working well. Ascorbic acid, better known as vitamin C, is important for maintaining your gums and soft tissues, and it may help fight infection and reduce the length and seriousness of common colds. Folacin helps your red blood cells divide and reproduce properly. Riboflavin, niacin, and thiamin are important for energy production in all of your body's cells. Vitamin B_6 helps your body make good use of protein. Vitamin B_{12} is important to help maintain normal red blood cells. Calcium and phosphorus are needed for bone growth and development. Iodine helps your body run at a proper rate so you're neither too tired or too peppy. Iron helps to maintain normal red blood cells. Magnesium helps with energy production in all your cells. Zinc is needed for overall normal growth and development and to allow you to taste foods properly.

AVERAGE HEIGHTS AND WEIGHTS AND RECOMMENDED ENERGY INTAKE

	Age (years)	Weight (pounds)	Height (inches)	Energy Needs (calories)	Energy Needs Range (calories)
Males	7–10	62	52	2400	(1650–3300)
	11–14	99	62	2700	(2000–3700)
	15–18	145	69	2800	(2100–3900)
	19–22	154	70	2900	(2500–3300)
Females	11–14	101	62	2200	(1500–3000)
	15–18	120	64	2100	(1200–3000)
	19–22	120	64	2100	(1700–2500)

Adapted from: National Research Council, National Academy of Sciences, *Recommended Dietary Allowances,* Ninth Edition, 1980, Washington, D.C.

RECOMMENDED VITAMIN AND MINERAL INTAKE

	Males		Females	
	11–14 years	15–18 years	11–14 years	15–18 years
weight (pounds)	99	145	101	120
height (inches)	62	69	62	64
Fat-Soluble Vitamins				
Vitamin A IU***	5000	5000	4000	4000
Vitamin D mcg**	10	10	10	10
Vitamin E mg*	8	10	8	8
Water-Soluble Vitamins				
Ascorbic Acid				
(Vitamin C) mg*	50	60	50	60
Folacin mcg**	400	400	400	400
Riboflavin mg*	1.6	1.7	1.3	1.3
Niacin mg****	18	18	15	14
Thiamin mg*	1.4	1.4	1.1	1.1
Vitamin B_6 mg*	1.8	2.0	1.8	2.0
Vitamin B_{12} mcg**	3.0	3.0	3.0	3.0
Minerals				
Calcium mg*	1200	1200	1200	1200
Phosphorus mg*	1200	1200	1200	1200
Iodine mg**	150	150	150	150
Iron mg*	18	18	18	18
Magnesium mg*	350	400	300	300
Zinc mg*	15	15	15	15

****milligrams of niacin equivalents
***international units
**micrograms
*milligrams

Adapted from: National Research Council, National Academy of Sciences, *Recommended Dietary Allowances,* Ninth Edition, 1980, Washington, D.C.

RICH SOURCES OF FAT-SOLUBLE AND WATER-SOLUBLE VITAMINS

Vitamin D

Fish, Liver, Oils
Fortified Milk
Exposure to Sunlight*
Butter

Phosphorus

Milk
Cheese
Ice Cream
Turnips and Mustard Greens
Collards, Kale, Broccoli
Canned Salmon, Sardines

Vitamin K

Fish, Liver, Oils
Butter
Ice Cream
Milk
Dark-Green Leafy Vegetables
Yellow Vegetables
Cheddar Cheese
Eggs
Yellow Fruits
Liver

Vitamin E

Wheat Germ Oil
Vegetable Oils
(Ex. Soybean, Corn, Cottonseed)
Nuts
Legumes

Iodine

Seafood
Iodized Salt

Vitamin B_{12}

Animal Products
Milk
Cheese
Eggs
Meat

Vitamin C

Oranges
Grapefruit
Tangerines
Strawberries
Cantaloupe
Tomatoes
Cabbage

Riboflavin

Milk
Meat
Eggs
Dark-Green Leafy Vegetables

*Partially activates vitamin D in
your skin tissue.

Folacin

Liver
Yeast
Dark-Green Leafy Vegetables
Whole Grain Cereal
Dry Beans

Vitamin B_6

Meats
Liver
Whole Grain Cereal
Soybeans
Peanuts
Corn
Potatoes
Dark-Green Leafy Vegetables
Wheat Germ

Magnesium

Bananas
Whole Grain Cereal
Dry Beans
Milk
Dark-Green Vegetables
Nuts

Zinc

Shellfish
Meat
Cheese
Whole Grain Cereal
Dry Beans
Cocoa
Nuts

Niacin

Animal Products
Whole Grain Cereal
Bread
Green Vegetables
Peanuts

Thiamin

Pork
Liver
Whole Grain Cereal
Bread
Soybeans
Peanuts
Milk

You should plan to include these essential nutrients in your daily diet. It's important to point out that research has identified over sixty nutrients your body needs to stay healthy—and there may be more. So a vitamin and mineral supplement with only a limited number of nutrients (say twelve) cannot replace all the foods that are rich in many nutrients. The key is to eat a balanced and varied diet. It's especially important to think a lot about nutrients during the teenage years because this is the time in your life when your needs are the greatest.

3

Personal Diet Needs

When someone mentions the word "diet," what thoughts first come to your mind? Do you get happy, pleasant thoughts? Chances are that when you think of a diet you get many unpleasant thoughts of boring foods and depriving yourself of your favorite treats.

You might look for a diet in a book or magazine or try the latest diet that your friends are following. Often such diets list what you should eat and what you shouldn't eat. They may give you menus for one or two weeks. The first few days are easy sailing. You may even feel proud and great that you're finally doing something about your weight. But how long does this last? How long can you make it without longing for some ice cream or pizza or some other favorite food? What's the problem with this way to weight management?

Many people have tried fad diets and sometimes have had short-term success. Unfortunately, most of those same people have not kept the weight off. When this happens people tend to feel badly. They also have a lot of feelings of guilt. A major shortcoming of many of the popular diets is that they don't teach people how to work in their favorite foods and still manage their weight. So, if you:

1. find the popular or fad diets boring and lacking your favorite foods;
2. dislike the rigid structure of diets or people telling you exactly what and what not to eat;
3. would like more freedom to work in your favorite foods;
4. would like to eat your favorites guilt-free;
5. want to avoid the on-and-off or "yo-yo" diet cycle;
6. want to feel more in control of your own food choices; and
7. want lasting success;

then read on! This book is designed for the kind of person who wants or feels all those things. How do you achieve them? Where do you start? Follow the four steps outlined in the rest of this chapter and you'll be on your way to success!

STEP 1
Keep an Eye Toward Success: Assess Your Readiness

How much do you want to change your eating habits? This experience should be positive and successful. You don't want to have either a first or yet another problem with weight management. Learning to manage your weight does take effort. But think about anything you ever learned. Learning to ride a bike, learning to play a new sport, all took time and effort. Sometimes you fell down or lost, but as long as you didn't give up because of the least little mistake and kept practicing, you became better and better at whatever it was you were learning.

Expect to spend about a half hour each day on learning about and changing your eating habits. Because of the time it takes to work on successful weight control, you need to consider what other things you're doing at the present time. If you already have too much to do— maybe a busy class schedule, a job after school, or band practice—it may not be the best time to work on your weight. That's okay. Wait until you can make weight-reduction efforts one of your Number One priorities. If you're willing to do that for the next two or three months, the odds are in your favor that you'll succeed now and forever.

How do you feel about the following statements?

1. I'm ready to devote the effort necessary to learn about and change my eating habits. I realize this may involve about a half hour each day.
2. Even with other school and social activities, I'll still be able to make weight management a Number One priority for at least two months.
3. I don't have any special medical problems that prevent me from undertaking my own weight-management program.
4. I realize that weight loss alone is not the answer to all other problems I may have. It's my weight, not my parents, teachers, or friends, that bothers me the most.
5. I'm willing to learn calorie values in order to work in my favorite foods.
6. I want to manage my weight because of *me* and not

because someone else wants me to or is pressuring me to lose weight.

7. I don't feel as if I have any extreme binge eating problems.

8. I have a positive outlook and expect myself to be eighty percent *not* one hundred percent successful. I'm not going to expect myself to be perfect.

9. I know that my weight management is my own responsibility. I expect there may be obstacles to overcome along the way, but I'm the one who puts the food in my mouth.

If you agree with most of these ideas, then it's probably the right time for you to diet.

STEP 2
Don't Go on Any Last Minute Binges or "Pig Out" on Your Favorite Foods

This book will teach you how to work in, plan for, and enjoy your favorite foods as you manage your weight and nutrient intake. No one will tell you, "Don't eat _____ because it's not on your diet." You won't be made to feel guilty for eating. This approach has helped thousands of people to successfully manage their weight.

If your family and friends know you're trying to control your weight, it might be helpful to tell them about this philosophy, which allows you to work in some of your favorite foods. This way they will be less likely to misjudge your eating behavior.

Know what your favorite foods are. List them in your diet notebook. These will be the food items that you can plan to eat when you have earned a calorie bonus.

STEP 3
Investigate and Gather Baseline Data

No two people are exactly alike. We're all individuals. The diet that works for one person may not work successfully for another. Each person must know his or her own needs. You must know your good points and habits as well as your bad ones.

Start a new page in your notebook to record this important information. Refer to the height and weight tables in Chapter 2 to help you.

1. Today's date:
2. My height is:
3. My height category for my age is:
4. My current weight is:
5. My weight category for my age is:
6. My chest measurement (across the nipples) is:
7. My waist measurement is:
8. My hip measurement is:
9. My thigh measurement is:
10. Now list good points and habits you have going for you. (Think about your eyes, hair, teeth, and other physical attributes. Are you a good dancer or an athlete?)

Keep a food record for the next seven days. Don't change your eating habits. Try not to eat more or less than usual. Look at the sample on page 39 and make forms of your own to use.

1. *Time of day:* Take a quick look at the clock, or at least make a good guess.

2. *Number of minutes spent eating:* Did your sandwich last two minutes or ten minutes?

3. *Where?:* This is the place you were at the time you were eating. Dining room table? Standing at the refrigerator?

4. *What else were you doing while eating?:* This is any other activity you were doing at the same time you were eating. Doing homework? Watching TV? Only eating?

5. *What were you thinking or feeling while eating?:* Describe what you were saying to yourself or what mood you were in. Were you nervous about an exam coming up in one hour? Were you relaxed?

6. *Food Quantity:*
   a. *Amount:* Use regular household measuring utensils or begin to read amounts from labels. There's a lot of information there and it only takes a minute to get it.
   b. *Calories:* Remember, all foods are allowed. Just look up the values.

7. *How much you enjoyed it:* If you ate this food item with great enjoyment, put a 1. If you ate this food with no real special enjoyment, it was just okay, put a 2. If you enjoyed only the first few bites, put a 3. If you really didn't enjoy it, put a 4. Remember, the diet in this book allows you to have your favorite foods.

STEP 4
Examine Your Records

This is day 8. Congratulations! Perhaps for the first time in your life you're getting praise for eating in your usual way. Nutrition experts and successful weight watchers realize how important it is to gather this baseline information. Without it, you wouldn't know what areas to work on.

Take your weight again. Write it down in your notebook. Any change? If so, record that change. If you stayed the same, then you're eating somewhere around the number of calories it takes to maintain your weight. If you gained, then you're eating more. If you lost, then you're probably eating less unless you changed your level of exercise.

Average your calories for the week. You can do this by writing down the number of calories you ate each day for the seven days (day 1 + day 2 + day 3 + day 4 + day 5 + day 6 + day 7 = total calories). Then take the seven-day total and divide by 7 to get your daily average (total calories divided by 7 = daily average).

Here's an example:

day 1: 1850 calories
day 2: 1700 calories
day 3: 1810 calories
day 4: 1600 calories
day 5: 1720 calories
day 6: 2000 calories
day 7: 2300 calories

1850 + 1700 + 1810 + 1600 + 1720 + 2000 + 2300 = 12,980 total calories for 7 days

12,980 ÷ 7 = 1854 daily average calories

Now you're ready to evaluate your record. Don't jump to conclusions about your habits; take time to consider all the points discussed below.

1. TIME OF DAY

Do you eat in a regular pattern each day? Does your eating pattern change from day to day? To gain the greatest control over your eating habits it's important to establish a regular pattern. Studies have shown that people have the greatest success with weight control when they eat a minimum of three times and up to six times per day. Skipping can cause extreme hunger that could lead to a binge or overeating.

If you need to have a more regular pattern, aim for gradual change. For example, if you eat breakfast once a week, aim next week for three times. The following week aim for five times. Your ultimate goal may be to eat breakfast six or seven times each week, but start out gradually.

What are your goals? Use the following sample statements to write your goals down in your diet notebook.

Currently I eat

    breakfast _____ times a week
    lunch _____ times a week
    dinner _____ times a week

Next week I'll gradually change this to eating

    breakfast _____ times a week
    lunch _____ times a week
    dinner _____ times a week

If I'm successful with this, the following week I'll eat

    breakfast _____ times a week
    lunch _____ times a week
    dinner _____ times a week

My final goal is to eat

breakfast	_____	times a week
lunch	_____	times a week
dinner	_____	times a week

If you already eat breakfast, lunch, and dinner at regular times, then the number of meals you eat is probably not a problem area for you. Think about between-meal eating. Do you have regular snacks between meals or after dinner? Do you get up at night and raid the fridge? If so, you may want to set goals to reduce the number of snacks *or* to change the type of snack. You may find that you enjoy your afternoon snack, but that you could choose better foods. Then in the coming weeks you could try to eat more nutritious foods instead of the junk you may be eating.

As you keep your weekly records, you may want to have a separate page in your notebook to keep a tally of the total number of breakfasts, lunches, dinners, and snacks you have eaten each week. Here is a sample you may want to use for your notebook:

Total breakfasts:	Total lunches:	Total snacks:	Total dinners:
week 1:	week 1:	week 1:	week 1:
week 2:	week 2:	week 2:	week 2:
week 3:	week 3:	week 3:	week 3:

2. NUMBER OF MINUTES SPENT EATING

Your body needs a chance to recognize its own sense of being full. Slow down. You'll eat less and feel just as full. Here are some tips to help you slow down:

TIP 1: Take smaller bites.

TIP 2: Put less food on your fork.

TIP 3: Put your fork or sandwich down between bites.

TIP 4: Take more time to concentrate on the taste; relax while you eat.

TIP 5: Allow time for your food to mix with your saliva—don't wash the food down with a beverage.

Do you eat too fast? If you do, write down your plans for how you will change this habit.

3. WHERE?

Be sure to look at where you eat meals as well as have your snacks. A certain place may be special to you. Each time you're there you may get hungry just because you're at that place!

Try to eat only at certain places that are especially designed for eating, such as kitchens and dining rooms. When possible, try to sit while you eat rather than stand. If you must bring something into the TV room, bring a small portion rather than the whole bag or box. If you eat at a place that's on your way home, change your route. Put temptation out of your path!

4. WHAT ELSE WERE YOU DOING WHILE EATING?

When you can, avoid distractions. It's best to make eating a separate activity. If you're eating cookies while doing your homework, you could eat a whole box before you know what you're doing! Here are some tips to break the activity-and-eating habit:

TIP 1: Eat and eat only. Don't eat just because you always do when you're studying or watching TV.

TIP 2: Talk more. You can't talk (very well at least) with food in your mouth.

TIP 3: Do activities that are difficult to do while you're eating such as playing a video game or knitting.

TIP 4: If you're not really hungry, delay eating by doing something else:
—call a friend
—look at old photos
—take a shower

Hunger pangs are usually short-lived and will go away in about fifteen minutes.

Is eating and doing something else at the same time a habit you need to change? If so, try to write down in your notebook your strategy for stopping this problem.

5. THOUGHTS, FEELINGS, MOODS, ENJOYMENT WHILE EATING

Do you enjoy the foods you eat? Do you use food as a treat? Do you eat when you're depressed? Think about it. Does eating really solve the problem? Or does it make you feel even worse if you overeat? What you say to yourself can affect your decisions!

It's Time to Summarize

In order to control your weight successfully, you've learned about your good eating habits and your problem eating habits. Now you must decide what you'd like to do. Read over this list. In your notebook, copy the items that apply to you.

1. Eat three regular meals.
2. Have planned snacks between meals.
3. Slow down my speed of eating.
4. Manage my environment.
5. Eat and eat only. Concentrate more on enjoying each bite.
6. Learn to delay my hunger by waiting at least fifteen minutes or getting involved in another activity.
7. Find a new reward or way to relax besides food.
8. Other (describe).

Daily Food Record For: _____ Day _____ Date _____, 19 _____

WHAT I ATE AND DRANK

Time of Day	Minutes Spent Eating	Where	Doing What Else	My thoughts, feelings, emotions, or moods	How much I enjoyed it: 1, 2, 3, 4	What	Amount	Calories	Total Calories for the day =

Diet How-to's

In Chapter 3 you were given an opportunity to assess your personal diet needs. Now you have reached the point where you should be ready to build your own healthful diet using the guidelines of the Lean Teen Tradeoff Diet Plan—The LTTD Approach—which is outlined in this chapter.

The **goals** of this diet plan are simple:

1. A leaner body.
2. A leaner and more healthy diet (that is, one lower in calories and lower in fat).
3. Dieting success without feeling deprived psychologically or being deprived nutritionally.

The **principles** of this diet are as follows:

1. Certain foods in your diet can be traded for each other because of the similar nutrient content.
2. You make the tradeoffs.
3. To stay balanced nutritionally, trade off only within groups.

4. Omitting groups or trying to make the diet any "leaner" will only destroy the nutritional content, and in the long run won't help you lose weight.

5. The diet includes lean meat, fish, and poultry. It's rich in natural, unprocessed foods and higher in fiber, starches, fruits, and vegetables, while leaner in saturated fats, cholesterol, and total fat.

6. Trade bonuses are provided for occasional fast foods and your favorites (yes, even a hot fudge sundae!). No food is forbidden. That's why there's a Tradeoff Bonus Category in the week's menus. This will add flexibility and let you control your own diet. You can use the bonus every day or save it up over a few days for a *big* bonus.

7. The rate of weight loss should be one to two pounds per week. A loss faster than this suggests that fluid (water) weight rather than body fat weight is causing the scale to tip downward. Too rapid a weight loss is easily regained just by drinking fluids. A steady loss of one or two pounds a week is *excellent* progress and ideal. If you aim to lose five or more pounds a week, like some fad dieters do, you're setting yourself up for problems; weight lost at this rate is easily gained back.

8. At a rate of one to two pounds per week, how long will it take you to reach your weight goal? When you size this up against how long it took you to put the weight on you'll see that it probably will take you less time to lose it than it did to gain it.

Remember, the LTTD goes hand in hand with an exercise program outlined in several other chapters in this book. While you're changing your eating habits, you should also be working on toning, firming, and improving your overall physical fitness. Both diet and exercise are the keys to the new lean and healthy you!

The LTTD Approach

The Lean Teen Tradeoff Diet is balanced and nutritionally sound. It was designed to avoid many of the pitfalls of a lopsided diet. You'll learn long-term principles of weight control and you'll be able to plan what your daily menus will be. There's a wide variety of foods from which you can plan your meals. Most importantly, you'll be encouraged to lose body fat rather than to lose weight quickly through a drastic drop in body fluids which may result in dehydration.

The LTTD Approach is based on a tradeoff system that can be carried on healthily for your entire life. There are nine tradeoff categories or food groups from which you will select the foods that will make up your daily menus. The tradeoff categories are as follows:

Nine Tradeoff Categories or Food Groups

1. **Lean Meat, Fish, and Poultry.** Excellent sources of protein, iron, zinc, vitamin B_{12} and other B complex vitamins. Lower in saturated fat and cholesterol than fattier meats, fish, poultry. Each 1-ounce serving contains approximately 55 calories.
2. **Egg, whole.** Classified separately due to its unique protein and cholesterol content. Because of its complete protein but higher cholesterol content, limit intake to two a week including eggs used in cooking

such as French toast, pancakes, pastries and cakes, and in salads such as egg salad. One egg contains about 75 calories.

3. **Low-fat (under 1%) and Non-fat Dairy Products.** Concentrated sources of calcium, phosphorus, protein, vitamin B_{12}, and folacin. Due to fortification practices they are also rich in vitamins A and D. One serving contains about 80 calories.

4. **Vegetable Oil and Soft Margarines and Nuts.** These foods help you feel full and provide essential fats. Each trade contains about 45 calories.

5. **Breads and Cereals and Whole Grain Cereal Products.** These are good sources of thiamin, iron, and in many cases dietary fiber. One tradeoff unit contains 70 calories.

6. **Fruits.** Citrus fruits and deep-red and yellow fruits such as strawberries and cantaloupes are good sources of vitamin C. Dried fruits are rich in vitamin A. One tradeoff unit contains 40 calories.

7. **Starchy Vegetables.** These are good sources of iron, and when combined with other foods such as milk, eggs, meat, and nuts, can provide complete protein. Their lower fat content makes them a good choice. One tradeoff unit contains about 70 calories.

8. **Other Vegetables.** These foods appeal to many senses because of their crispness when fresh (hear the snap), colorful variety, and varied texture (they crunch, snap in your mouth). Their relatively low calorie content (25 calories per trade) means they can be planned into the diet frequently. Their variety and appeal expand the combinations of food you can have while dieting. Build a "Dagwood" sandwich with lean meat or fish or poultry, and add in sprouts, shredded lettuce, grated carrots, slices of tomatoes, lettuce, and other

veggies. Put everything in a "pocket," whole grain pouch, or other whole grain bread. Keep these foods on hand for snacking. In addition to their sensuous appeal, the deep-green and yellow vegetables provide vitamin A, while the deep greens are also good sources of vitamin C. A variety of vegetables adds potassium, folacin, and vitamin B_6 too.

9. **Sugar, Sweets, and Higher Fat Foods.** To neglect mentioning these foods would not be fair. Let's face it, they're part of the American diet. The key to reaching and maintaining your weight goal is to keep these items in check, to work on a *planned* bonus trade. These foods may provide certain nutrients; however, their major contribution is calories and possibly fat. Be reasonable.

Occasionally, you will want to splurge on fast foods. Refer to the calorie charts in the appendix and the tradeoff charts in this chapter to determine how to make your trades.

Seven Steps to Success

You now have some of the background information needed to help you better understand the LTTD Approach. In this section you'll read about the seven steps you need to follow to put this dietary plan into practice.

STEP 1
Setting Your Calorie Level

First you must pick an appropriate calorie level to maintain your weight, or if you need to lose some weight, pick a weight-reduction calorie level. Here's how to do it.

Weight Maintenance

To *maintain* your bodyweight, assuming you do a moderate amount of exercise, for *females,* you would follow this formula:

Females: current weight (lbs) × 17 = calories per day

This means if a female currently weighs 100 pounds, she would multiply 100 by 17 to get 1700 calories per day, which she would eat to keep her weight the same. Remember, this formula assumes that she is doing a moderate amount of exercise each day.

For *males,* the formula is:

Males: current weight (lbs) × 20 = calories per day

This means if a male weighs 200 pounds, he would multiply 200 by 20 to get 4000 calories per day, which he would eat to keep his weight the same. Remember, this formula assumes that he is also doing a moderate amount of exercise each day.

Weight Reduction

To *lose* weight, again assuming you do a moderate amount of exercise, for *females* you would follow this formula:

FEMALES:
ideal body weight × 10 = calories per day

This means that first the female must determine her ideal bodyweight, which she can do by using the information from the height and weight charts in Chapter 2, and then multiply by 10 to get the total number of calories she would be able to eat each day and still lose weight safely.

For *males* the formula is:

MALES:
ideal body weight $\times$ 12 = calories per day

This means that first the male must determine his ideal bodyweight, which he can do by using the information from the height and weight charts in Chapter 2, and then multiply by 12 to get the total number of calories he would be able to eat each day and still lose weight safely.

STEP 2
Adjusting Your Calorie Level

You only need to follow the instructions in this step if you're *very physically active*. The purpose of step 2 is to adjust the calorie level you just calculated in step 1 to keep it in tune with your exercise level. If you do more than moderate exercise, your body will need to take in more calories so it will be able to function properly. If you think you do need to adjust your calorie level, here's how to do it.

First you must estimate the number of minutes you exercise daily by the type of activity. For example, if you run for 15 minutes in the morning and 15 minutes again in the afternoon, you would estimate that you spend about 30 minutes per day running. Then you need to calculate the calorie value of the exercise. In the example noted above, running for 30 minutes uses about 300 calories. The charts in Chapter 5 listing the calorie values of many common exercises will help you with these calculations. Finally, you need to take the calorie values of the exercises and add them to the calorie level you estimated in step 1.

Pretend for a moment that Susan Smith is your classmate. She has just decided to go on the Lean Teen Tradeoff Diet Plan. After looking at the height and weight charts in Chapter 2, Susan has decided that her ideal weight is 120 pounds. Because Susan now weighs about 125 pounds, she has decided to use the formula in step 1 that's for weight reduction. Her weight reduction formula looks like this:

ideal weight (120 lbs) × 10 = 1200 calories per day

But Susan feels that she does more than a moderate amount of exercise each day. In fact, Susan runs for about 20 minutes each day and plays tennis for about 30 minutes each day. So Susan decides that she needs to follow the directions in step #2 to adjust her calorie level.

Susan's calorie level from

step 1	1200 calories
20 minutes running	+ 300 calories
30 minutes tennis	+ 200 calories
adjusted calorie level	= 1700 calories

For Susan to lose weight safely, she can eat about 1700 calories each day. Keep Susan's case in mind as you follow the rest of the steps in the LTTD Approach.

STEP 3
Organizing Your Trades

Now that you've figured out how many calories you may eat each day, you're ready to determine how you'll organize your diet to stay within that calorie amount. You'll need the Organizing Trades chart in this chapter to help you complete this part of the diet plan.

The Organizing Trades chart is divided into three major parts around the three main meals that you'll eat each day: breakfast, lunch, and dinner. Under each meal you'll find the eight important food groups listed. The ninth food group, sugars, sweets, and other high-fat foods, is of high caloric content and isn't included on the chart; however, you may select such foods if you wish as part of your bonus calories. Please note that bonus calories are listed only once at the end of the chart and may be used each day or saved for a special larger bonus at another time during a one-week period.

The numbers that appear across the top of the chart are daily calorie levels like the ones you determined in steps 1 and 2 of this dietary plan. The numbers inside the chart are the number of trade units or portions that you're allowed to eat within each food group and each calorie level.

The best way to use this chart is first to pick out one calorie level. Think back to your imaginary classmate Susan Smith. After she completed step 2, Susan figured out that she should eat 1700 calories a day to lose weight safely. Put your finger on the 1700 calorie level at the top of the chart. To determine how many trade units in each food group Susan can make for each meal, you'll just

LEAN TEEN TRADEOFF DIET
ORGANIZING TRADES

Note: Numbers within the chart refer to how many portions of food within that food group you are allowed to eat, or trades you are allowed to make.

	Calorie Levels						
	1200	1300	1400	1500	1600	1700	1800
Breakfast Food Groups							
1. meat, fish, poultry	—	—	—	—	—	—	—
2. egg, whole			about two per week				
3. dairy	1	1	1	1	1	1	1
4. oil, margarine, nuts	1	1	1	1	1	1	1
5. breads or cereals	1	1	2	2	2	2	2
6. fruits	1	1	1	1	2	2	2
7. starchy vegetables	—	—	—	—	—	—	—
8. vegetables	—	—	—	—	—	—	—
Lunch Food Groups							
1. meat, fish, poultry	2	2	2	2	3	3	3
2. egg, whole	—	—	—	—	—	—	—
3. dairy	½	½	½	½	½	½	½
4. oil, margarine, nuts	1	1	1	1	1	2	2
5. breads or cereals	2	2	2	2	2	2	2
6. fruits	1	2	2	2	2	2	2
7. starchy vegetables	—	—	—	—	—	—	—
8. vegetables	1	1	1	2	2	2	2
Dinner Food Groups							
1. meat, fish, poultry	3	4	4	4	4	4	4
2. egg, whole	—	—	—	—	—	—	—
3. dairy	½	½	½	½	½	½	½
4. oil, margarine, nuts	1	1	2	2	2	2	3
5. breads or cereals	1	1	1	1	1	2	2
6. fruits	1	1	1	1	1	1	1
7. starchy vegetables	—	—	—	1	1	1	1
8. vegetables	2	2	2	2	2	2	2
Snack Fruit	1	1	1	1	1	1	2
Bonus Calories*	100	100	100	100	100	100	100

*Bonus calories can be added to meals, used as snacks, or saved up over time for a splurge.

follow the 1700 calorie column all the way down. If you do this correctly, you'll find the following:

Susan's Breakfast:

Food Groups	Trade Units
meat, fish, poultry	0
egg, whole	(2 per week)
dairy	1
oil, margarine, nuts	1
breads or cereals	2
fruits	2
starchy vegetables	0
vegetables	0

Susan's Lunch:

Food Groups	Trade Units
meat, fish, poultry	3
egg, whole	0
dairy	1/2
oil, margarine, nuts	2
breads or cereals	2
fruits	2
starchy vegetables	0
vegetables	2

Susan's Dinner:

Food Groups	Trade Units
meat, fish, poultry	4
egg, whole	0
dairy	1/2
oil, margarine, nuts	2

Food Groups	*Trade Units*
breads or cereals	2
fruits	1
starchy vegetables	1
vegetables	2
Susan's Snack Fruit	1
Susan's Bonus Calories	100 calories

Susan can follow this plan or she can change it a little. Susan can add up the total number of trade units she is allowed in each food group for a whole day. Those numbers would look like this:

Food Groups	*Trade Units*
meat, fish, poultry	7
egg, whole	(2 per week)
dairy	2
oil, margarine, nuts	5
breads or cereals	6
fruits	6
starchy vegetables	1
vegetables	4
Bonus Calories	100 calories

As long as Susan eats the correct number of trade units from each food group each day, she can eat them at any meal or snacktime that she chooses. That's why this is called a tradeoff diet!

So Susan has a choice of using the trade units for breakfast, lunch, dinner, and snacks as shown on the chart, or she may design her own special way to use this information. Here's a sample of how Susan might decide to use her trade units on one day:

1700 CALORIES

Trade Category	Breakfast # Trades	Lunch # Trades	P.M. Snack # Trades	Dinner # Trades
meat, fish, poultry	—	3	—	4
dairy	1	—	1/2	1/2
oil, margarine, nuts	1	2	1	1
breads or cereals	2	2	1	1
fruits	1	2	2	1
starchy vegetables	—	—	—	1
vegetables	—	1	1	2
Bonus		100 Calories		

The choice is really up to Susan to make. But it's good to keep in mind that a three-meal-a-day plan with a snack is the best for maintaining weight loss.

Now it's your turn to organize your trades. Find the level of calories you estimate you need every day on the Organizing Trades chart. That calorie estimate should come from step 1 or 2 of this chapter. Next, look at the number of servings or trade units allowed per meal from each of the eight trading groups. Then decide how you want to use those trades for breakfast, lunch, dinner, and snacks. Make a sample chart of your choice so you'll know what to follow when you come to step 4, Planning Your Meals. Put this information in your log.

STEP 4
Planning Your Meals

You should begin to plan your meals by thinking of trade units. Each trade unit that you're allowed to eat comes from a food group. Each food group contains many different things to eat. For example, in the meat, fish, and poultry food group there are various cuts of beef, lamb, pork, veal, chicken, turkey, and fish. These different foods all have different caloric contents, but each trade unit is supposed to be worth the same number of calories. So, the amount of food you're allowed to eat for each trade unit will depend on which foods you select. For example, in the meat, fish, and poultry food group, each trade should be equal to about 55 calories. That means if you select tuna, you are allowed ¼ cup, but if you select lean hamburger, you're allowed only 1 ounce of meat per one trade unit.

At the end of this chapter you'll find a Trade Units chart. Each of the eight important food groups is listed separately. The number of calories allowed per trade unit within each food group is noted right beside the food group name. Under each heading you'll find a wide variety of foods listed that you may select for your trade units. Beside each food listing you'll find the amount of that food that is allowed to equal one trade for that particular food group.

Take a moment now to turn to the Trade Units chart at the end of this chapter. Look at food group 1. How many calories per trade are you allowed to eat for food group 1? The answer should be about 55 calories per trade. How much shrimp would you be allowed to eat to equal one trade or 55 calories? The answer is 5 pieces or 1 ounce. Look through some of the other food groups. Be sure you understand how to use this chart before you start planning your meals.

When you're ready to begin to plan your daily menu, try to choose a variety of foods from the trade units described on the charts at the end of this chapter. Your goal should be to prepare a balanced, healthy, lean menu plan.

Don't forget! One of the most exciting parts of this diet **is** that you can make tradeoffs. You also have opportuni**tie**s to make bonus calorie trades.

Tradeoffs

Even tradeoffs—that is, switches within the same food **group** for the same amount of calories—are easy to do. **Here**'s an example. Your breakfast menu lists a slice of whole wheat bread (70 calories). The blueberry muffin (small) in the breadbox looks very tempting (70 calories). This is an even trade. Go on and enjoy that muffin!

How do you do a trade for a bonus category? Here's an example. You are following the 1200-calorie plan and know you and your friends are planning to stop at your favorite hangout on the weekend. Maybe you'd like a small Coke and fries. Save up your bonus calories for 3 days, 300 calories, and you're all set. What about a hot fudge sundae (1 cup ice cream = 260 calories, 1/4 cup hot fudge = 250 calories, 2 1/2 tablespoons whipped cream = 165 calories: total = 675 calories)? Save your bonuses for the weekend treat! (A listing of the fast food and snack trades can be found in the appendix. In addition, you'll also find there a chart of the caloric values **of** common foods. Use this information to add flexibility and fun to your diet plans.)

Important Tradeoff Reminders

Due to their more concentrated calorie content and possibly higher fat content, use the following only in small quantities, only once in a while, and as Tradeoff Bonus foods. Refer to their calorie content to figure out how to trade off.

Peanut butter
Creamed cottage cheese
Soft cheeses like ricotta
Hard cheeses like cheddar
Cold cuts and frankfurters
Ground beef, including commercial hamburgers
Margarine or butter
Bacon
Cream—all types
Commercial salad dressing, except those made with corn, safflower, sunflower, soybean, and cottonseed oil
Mayonnaise and salad dressing
Whole milk and whole milk products, including whole milk yogurt
Cakes, pies, pastries—all types
Ice cream
Candies—all types

To help get you started, you might want to look at the following sample of a one-week menu plan that allows 1500 calories per day. If this is the correct calorie level for you, you might want to follow this diet for a week. Remember, because this is a tradeoff diet, you can swap any breakfast with any breakfast, any lunch with any lunch, and any dinner with any dinner.

Nutrition Plan for One Week

1500 CALORIES

BREAKFAST

TRADES
1 dairy
1 egg 2 times a week
1 oil, margarine, nuts
2 breads or cereals
1 fruit

DAY 1

Orange juice or fruit trade	½ cup
Scrambled egg	1
Whole wheat toast	2 slices
Margarine, soft	1 teaspoon
Skim milk	1 cup
Optional: Coffee, tea (regular or decaffeinated)	

DAY 2

Cantaloupe (½) or fruit trade	1
Shredded wheat cereal, large biscuit	1
Skim milk	1 cup
Optional: Coffee, tea (regular or decaffeinated)	

DAY 3

Grapefruit or fruit trade	½
Cheerios	¾ cup
Whole grain toast	1 slice
Margarine, soft	1 teaspoon
Skim milk	1 cup
Optional: Coffee, tea (regular or decaffeinated)	

DAY 4

Sliced peaches or fruit trade	½ cup
Whole grain pancakes	1½
Margarine	1 teaspoon
Diet maple syrup	
Skim milk	1 cup
Optional: Coffee, tea (regular or decaffeinated)	

DAY 5

Berries or fruit trade	½ cup
Corn muffin	1 whole
Bran flakes	½ cup
Skim milk	1 cup
Optional: Coffee, tea (regular or decaffeinated)	

DAY 6

Tomato juice or fruit trade	½ cup
Boiled egg	1
English muffin	1 whole
Margarine, soft	1 teaspoon
Optional: Coffee, tea (regular or decaffeinated)	

DAY 7

Pineapple chunks (own juice)	¹/₂ cup
Bagel	1
Cream cheese	1 tablespoon
Skim milk	1 cup
Optional: Coffee, tea (regular or decaffeinated)	

LUNCH

TRADES
2 ounces meat, fish, poultry
¹/₂ dairy
1 oil, margarine, nuts
2 breads or cereals
2 fruits
2 vegetables (non-starchy)

DAY 1

Tuna packed in water	¹/₂ cup
Whole grain bread	2 slices
Mayonnaise	1 teaspoon
Shredded vegetables	
lettuce	1 cup
carrot	¹/₂ cup
tomato	¹/₂ cup
Apple	1 medium
Skim milk	¹/₂ cup

DAY 2

Turkey	2 ounces
Whole wheat Syrian pouch	1
Mayonnaise	1 teaspoon
Lettuce	as desired
Sliced tomato	$1/2$ cup
Sprouts	$1/2$ cup
Fruit trade	2
Skim milk	$1/2$ cup

DAY 3

Peanut butter and banana sandwich	
Peanut butter	1 tablespoon
Banana	1 medium
Whole wheat bread	2 slices
Shredded vegetables	2 cups
Skim milk	$1/2$ cup

DAY 4

Salad bar	
Chick peas	$1/2$ cup
Mixed greens	1 cup
Sesame bread sticks	3
Vinegar and oil	1 teaspoon
Fruit trade	2
Skim milk	$1/2$ cup

DAY 5

Fast-food hamburger	1
French fries, small	1
Diet beverage	

DAY 6

Low-fat vanilla, coffee, or lemon yogurt	1 cup
Berries or fruit trade	2
Banana nut muffin	1 whole
Margarine	1 teaspoon

DAY 7

Chicken Sandwich	
Chicken	2 ounces
Whole grain bread	2 slices
Mayonnaise	1 teaspoon
Shredded vegetables	2 cups
Fruit trade	2

DINNER

TRADES	
Meat, fish, poultry	4 ounces
Dairy	1/2
Oil, margarine, nuts	2
Breads or cereals	1
Fruits	1
Starchy Vegetables	1
Vegetables	2

DAY 1

Broiled Beef (lean)	4 ounces
Baked potato	1 medium

Margarine	2 teaspoons
Broccoli	1 cup
Fruit trade	1
Skim milk	1/2 cup

DAY 2

Baked fish	4 ounces
Lima beans	1/2 cup
Sliced tomato	1
Whole wheat roll	1 whole
Margarine	2 teaspoons
Fruit trade	1
Skim milk	1/2 cup

DAY 3

Broiled chicken breast, no skin	4 ounces
Corn	2/3 cup
Tossed salad	1 1/2 cups
Homemade low-calorie dressing	2 tablespoons
Fruit trade	1
Skim milk	1/2 cup

DAY 4

Lasagna	1 cup
Leafy salad	1 1/2 cups
Green beans	1/2 cup
Fruit trade	1
Skim milk	1/2 cup

DAY 5

Lean roast pork	4 ounces
Sweet potato	1/2 cup
Whole wheat roll	1 whole
Margarine	2 teaspoons
Brussels sprouts	1 cup
Fruit trade	1
Skim milk	1/2 cup

DAY 6

Oriental stir fry	
Lean beef	4 ounces
Pea pods	3/4 cup
Rice (cooked)	1/2 cup
Bamboo shoots	1/4 cup
Sliced celery	1/4 cup
Sliced onion	1/4 cup
Oil	2 teaspoons
Fruit trade	1
Skim milk	1/2 cup

DAY 7

1/2 10" Thin-crust cheese pizza	
Skim milk	1/2 cup
Fruit trade	1

The information you acquired after steps 1, 2, and 3 of this plan needs to be put into your log. If you haven't already done so, take the time to do it now. Then you're ready to plan your meals. Go slowly at first. Don't be afraid to change your mind and trade one food for another. Just do your trades within a given food group and calorie level. The bonus category is for splurges!

STEP 5
Measuring Your Food

In order to properly use the LTTD Approach, you need to measure the portions of food you eat or read the food labels to check the weight of each serving size. Be sure to measure meats and rice after cooking because meat shrinks and rice expands. You can expect meat to shrink between 20 percent and 25 percent after it's cooked. So a 4-ounce serving of meat will become only 3 ounces after it's cooked. Rice will often expand to 2 to 3 times its size after it's cooked. So 1 cup of rice will often become 2 or 3 cups of rice after cooking.

Don't be afraid to ask for the sizes of the portions that are served to you in restaurants. This information will help you stay on your diet even while eating out.

STEP 6
Judging a Restaurant

Stop judging a restaurant by how *much* food they give you. Judge, instead, how *good* the food actually is.

STEP 7
Keeping a Record

Keep a record of your weight-loss progress. Be sure also to keep track of your weight-maintenance progress. The sample charts in Chapter 3 will help you do this in your own log book.

If you follow the seven steps to success as suggested in this chapter, you're on your way to a new and healthful way of eating that can be practiced for the rest of your life.

Dieter's Dilemma

Lose five pounds in five days! Take off unwanted inches *fast!* You've probably seen a great many diets that make such promises. No matter how smart you may be it's hard not to be attracted to such claims if you want to lose weight. It's easy to be taken in by a claim that makes dieting seem quick and easy.

But what's the difference between all those diets you see in books and magazines and the Lean Teen Tradeoff Diet? You may notice that some diets tell you to eat as much meat, chicken, or fish as you want as long as you don't let a morsel of bread or sweets pass your lips. Others may be labeled as a cleansing routine and suggest you drink only water and small amounts of freshly squeezed fruit juices and vegetable broths. Yet others emphasize more of a mix among meats, milk, breads, starches, fruits, and vegetables.

Does one diet work better than another? What happens to the body when these three different kinds of diets are followed for about eight to ten days? Do people lose more fat, more water, or more lean muscle tissue?

These same questions led two researchers from Columbia University College of Physicians and Surgeons and St. Luke's Hospital in New York to do an interesting study about weight loss and short-term (eight to ten days) dieting. They looked at the three kinds of diets mentioned above: a diet high in meats but low in starches and sugars; a fasting or starvation diet like what some fad dieters call a cleansing diet; and a diet that included a balanced mixture of all foods. The researchers were interested in finding out not only which diet caused the fastest drop on the scale, but also where (fat, muscle, or water) the actual weight loss came from. They found that the high-meat, low-starch diet and the starvation diets resulted in a somewhat faster weight loss for the short term, but most of the weight loss was from water, not fat. Water weight loss is quickly regained when eating habits return to normal, so the weight loss is not permanent. On the other hand, the diet that was a mixture of all food groups resulted in the least amount of fluid loss and more weight loss from fat. In other words, the balanced diet helps the dieter lose fat, not more muscle tissue or water. Thus, the Lean Teen Tradeoff Diet will maximize your chances for a permanent weight loss.

A Final Note

Part of becoming a successful dieter is learning to be a wise shopper. You'll also need to learn how to read food labels. The tips outlined below should help.

SHOPPING TIPS

TIP 1: Hunt for foods that are lower in fat, especially saturated fat, sugar, and eggs.

TIP 2: When foods contain fat, look for the following polyunsaturated ingredients: corn oil, safflower oil, sesame seed oil, and soy oil. Look for soft tub margarines. These are better for you.

TIP 3: Cheeses are usually high in fat. Some have as much as fifty percent or more of their calories in fat.

TIP 4: When you add ingredients to a product you buy, make sure it is "lean," such as nonfat or less than one percent fat dairy products. (Don't be afraid to ask your supermarket manager!)

Understanding Food Labels

Any food that has a nutrient added or that makes a nutritional claim (example: low in fat and cholesterol or sugar-free) must have a nutrition label. Many food companies voluntarily label foods.

Nutrition Label Information

1. **Serving size** This is the amount of food that is considered a reasonable serving (for example, one cup).
2. **Number of servings** in the container.
3. **Major nutrients** The label tells you the *amount* of calories, protein, carbohydrate, and fat per serving. The *type* of carbohydrate and fat is usually *not given*. Check the ingredient list on the product. All ingredients are listed in order of their concentration. (For example, if the first ingredient on the label is sugar, that means that a large amount of the carbohydrate in the food comes from sugar.)

Carbohydrate, protein, and fat. These are listed in grams. To change these amounts to calories, do the following:

For *carbohydrates*, take the listing in grams and multiply that number by 4. That will tell you how many calories of carbohydrates are in the food.

For *protein*, take the listing in grams and also multiply that number by 4. That will tell you how many calories of protein are in the food.

For *fat*, take the listing in grams and multiply that number by 9. That will tell you how many calories of fat are in the food.

Note: Fats have 2½ times the number of calories per gram than do protein and carbohydrates.

Vitamins and Minerals. The label gives the percentage of the U.S. Recommended Daily Allowance (USRDA) of selected nutrients. The standard USRDA most often used (an exception would be on baby foods) is the standard for a healthy adult male. It is often higher than the levels needed for many people. Your *total* daily intake, on the average usual day, should reach about 100 percent of the USRDA.

Cholesterol. Often the label contains information about cholesterol (per 100 grams or about a 3½-ounce serving), the total amount (percentage of the product from fat), and the type of fat (in grams, either saturated or polyunsaturated fat). Look for foods lower in cholesterol and saturated fat.

Sodium. The label may also contain information about sodium (salt) level. This is listed per 100 grams of food just as cholesterol is listed.

TRADE UNITS

FOOD GROUP 1:
LEAN MEAT, FISH, POULTRY (ABOUT 55 CALORIES PER TRADE)

Beef: Baby Beef (very lean), Chipped Beef, Chuck, Flank Steak, Tenderloin, Plate Ribs, Plate Skirt Steak, Round (bottom, top), All cuts Rump, Sirloin, Tripe	1 ounce
Lamb: Leg, Rib, Sirloin, Loin (roast and chops), Shank, Shoulder	1 ounce
Pork: Leg (whole rump, center shank), Ham, Smoked (center slices)	1 ounce
Veal: Leg, Loin, Rib, Shank, Shoulder, Cutlets	1 ounce
Poultry: Meat, without skin, of Chicken, Turkey, Cornish Hen, Pheasant	1 ounce
Fish: Any fresh or frozen	1 ounce
Canned Salmon, Tuna, Mackerel, Crab, Lobster	1/4 cup
Clams, Oysters, Scallops, Shrimp	5 pieces or 1 ounce
Sardines, drained	3 pieces
Cheeses: Containing less than 5% butterfat	1 ounce
Cottage Cheese: Dry and 2% butterfat	1/4 cup
Dried Beans and Peas (omit 1 bread trade)	1/2 cup

FOOD GROUP 2:
EGG (ABOUT 75 CALORIES PER TRADE)

Use only *2* per week either at a meal or in recipes.

FOOD GROUP 3:
DAIRY (ABOUT 80 CALORIES PER TRADE)

Preferred: Non-fat Fortified Milk	
Skim or non-fat milk	1 cup
Powdered (non-fat dry, before adding liquid)	1/3 cup

Canned, evaporated—skim milk	½ cup
Buttermilk made from skim milk	1 cup
Yogurt made from skim milk (plain, unflavored)	1 cup

Low-Fat Fortified Milk
1% Fat-fortified milk (omit ½ fat trade)	1 cup
2% Fat-fortified milk (omit 1 fat trade)	1 cup
Yogurt made from 2% fortified milk (plain, unflavored) (omit 1 fat trade)	1 cup

Occasional: Whole Milk (omit 2 fat trades)
Whole Milk	1 cup
Canned, evaporated whole milk	½ cup
Buttermilk made from whole milk	1 cup
Yogurt made from whole milk (plain, unflavored)	1 cup

FOOD GROUP 4:
FATS, OIL, MARGARINE, NUTS (ABOUT 45 CALORIES PER TRADE)

Preferred:
*Margarine, soft, tub, or stick	1 teaspoon
Avocado (4″ diameter)	⅛
Oil, Corn, Cottonseed, Safflower, Soy, Sunflower	1 teaspoon
Oil, Olive	1 teaspoon
Oil, Peanut	1 teaspoon
Olives	5 small
Almonds	10 whole
Pecans	2 large whole
Peanuts	
Spanish	20 whole
Virginia	10 whole
Walnuts	6 small
Nuts, Other	6 small

Occasional:
Margarine, regular stick	1 teaspoon
Butter	1 teaspoon
Bacon Fat	1 teaspoon
Bacon, crisp	1 strip

*made with corn, cottonseed, soy, or sunflower oil only

Cream, light	2 tablespoons
Cream, heavy	1 tablespoon
Cream, sour	2 tablespoons
Cream Cheese	1 tablespoon
French dressing	1 tablespoon
Italian dressing	1 tablespoon
Lard	1 teaspoon
Mayonnaise	1 teaspoon
Salt Pork	³/₄-inch cube

FOOD GROUP 5:
BREADS AND CEREALS (ABOUT 70 CALORIES PER TRADE)

Preferred:

Bread

White (including French and Italian)	1 slice
Whole Wheat	1 slice
Rye or Pumpernickel	1 slice
Raisin	1 slice
Bagel, small	¹/₂
English Muffin, small	¹/₂
Plain Roll, bread	1
Frankfurter Roll	¹/₂
Hamburger Bun	¹/₂
Dried Bread Crumbs	3 tablespoons
Tortilla, 6″	1

Cereal

Bran Flakes	¹/₂ cup
Other ready-to-eat unsweetened cereal	³/₄ cup
Puffed cereal (unfrosted)	1 cup
Cereal (cooked)	¹/₂ cup
Grits (cooked)	¹/₂ cup
Rice or Barley (cooked)	¹/₂ cup
Pasta (cooked) spaghetti, noodles, macaroni	¹/₂ cup
Popcorn (popped, no fat added)	3 cups
Cornmeal (dry)	2 tablespoons
Flour	2¹/₂ tablespoons
Wheat Germ	¹/₄ cup

Crackers

Arrowroot	3
Graham, 2½″ square	2
Matzo, 4″ × 6″	½
Oyster	20
Pretzels, 3⅛″ long × ⅛″ diameter	25
Rye Wafers, 2″ × 3½″	3
Saltines	6
Soda, 2½″ square	4

Occasional:

Prepared Foods

*Biscuit, 2″ diameter (omit 1 fat trade)	1
*Corn Bread, 2″ × 2″ × 1″ (omit 1 fat trade)	1
*Corn Muffin, 2″ diameter (omit 1 fat trade)	1
Crackers, round butter type (omit 1 fat trade)	5
*Muffin, plain, small (omit 1 fat trade)	1
Potatoes, French Fried, length 2″ to 3½″ (omit 1 fat trade)	8
Potato or Corn Chips (omit 2 fat trades)	15
*Pancakes, 5″ × ½″ (omit 1 fat trade)	1
*Waffle, 5″ × ½″ (omit 1 fat trade)	1

FOOD GROUP 6:
FRUITS (ABOUT 40 CALORIES PER TRADE)

Apple	1 small
Apple Juice	⅓ cup
Applesauce (unsweetened)	½ cup
Apricots (fresh)	2 medium
Apricots (dried)	4 halves
Banana	½ small

Berries

Blackberries	½ cup
Blueberries	½ cup
Raspberries	½ cup
Strawberries	¾ cup

*Experiment with your recipes and substitute soft margarine and preburned oils.

Cherries	10 large
Cider	1/3 cup
Dates	2
Figs (fresh)	1
Figs (dried)	1
Grapefruit	1/2
Grapefruit Juice	1/2 cup
Grapes	12
Grape Juice	1/4 cup
Mango	1/2 small

Melons

Cantaloupe	1/4 small
Honeydew	1/8 medium
Watermelon	1 cup

Nectarine	1 small
Orange	1 small
Orange Juice	1/2 cup
Papaya	3/4 cup
Peach	1 medium
Pear	1 small
Persimmon (native)	1 medium
Pineapple	1/2 cup
Pineapple Juice	1/3 cup
Plums	2 medium
Prunes	2 medium
Prune Juice	1/4 cup
Raisins	2 tablespoons
Tangerine	1 medium

FOOD GROUP 7:
STARCHY VEGETABLES (ABOUT 70 CALORIES PER TRADE)

Corn	1/3 cup
Corn on Cob	1 small
Lima Beans	1/2 cup
Parsnips	2/3 cup
Peas, Green (canned or frozen)	1/2 cup
Potato, White	1 small
Potato, Mashed	1/2 cup

Pumpkin	¾ cup
Winter Squash: Acorn, or Butternut	½ cup
Yam or Sweet Potato	¼ cup

Dried Beans, Peas, and Lentils

Beans, Peas, Lentils (dried and cooked)	½ cup
Baked Beans, no pork	¼ cup

FOOD GROUP 8:
VEGETABLES (ABOUT 25 CALORIES PER TRADE)

½ cup for the following vegetable trades:

Asparagus	Broccoli	Carrots
Bean Sprouts	Brussels Sprouts	Cauliflower
Beets	Cabbage	Celery
Eggplant	Mushrooms	Vegetable Juice
Green Pepper	Okra	Zucchini

Greens:

Beets	Onions
Chard	Rhubarb
Collards	Rutabaga
Dandelion	Sauerkraut
Kale	String Beans, Green or Yellow
Mustard	Summer Squash
Spinach	Tomatoes
Turnip	Tomato Juice

Use as much as you like of the following vegetables:

Chicory	Lettuce
Chinese Cabbage	Parsley
Endive	Radishes
Escarole	Watercress

SOURCE:
Adapted from the American Dietetic Association Meal Planning with Exchanges, Chicago, 1978.

5

Personal Fitness Needs

Are you physically fit? Would an exercise and/or weight-reduction program be right for you at this time? What goals would be best? Are you asking for something that will be impossible to do?

After you read the guidelines in this chapter for determining your present level of physical fitness, you'll have a chance to complete your own fitness profile worksheet. From the information you compile, you'll then be ready to design your own fitness program. Remember that good nutrition and exercise together can lead you to a lean teen body and a plan for overall fitness for your whole life!

What Is Physical Fitness?

If you're physically fit, you should have enough energy to do your everyday tasks. You should also have enough energy left over to have fun and enjoyment with your friends.

Physical fitness is made up of the following five important categories: flexibility, muscular strength, muscular endurance, motor ability, and cardiorespiratory endurance. You must be fit in each area if you want to be physically fit.

Flexibility helps your body move smoothly without any unnecessary awkwardness. Technically it's explained as the range of motion at a joint or groups of joints. Walking is a simple skill that requires flexibility. A tennis serve or a cartwheel is more difficult, but also requires flexibility.

Muscular strength helps you lift groceries, carry books, chop wood, move furniture, and even run to catch a bus. It's explained as the ability of a muscle to produce force against a resistance in one big contraction. Think of arm wrestling with a friend. Your friend's arm is a force you must overcome or resist. This activity requires you to have muscular strength.

There are two kinds of *muscular endurance*. Raking leaves, washing the floor, swimming, and doing push-ups are all examples of isotonic exercise. Carrying a load of books for a few minutes or holding any heavy object for a while are examples of isometric exercise. Isometric exercise is described as the ability of a muscle to perform work by holding a muscular contraction. Isotonic exercise is the ability of a muscle to perform work by continuing to raise and lower relatively heavy loads.

Persons with talent in gymnastics, all racquet sports, skating, and skiing have superior *motor ability*. Motor ability is a person's ability to perform various physical skills well, that is, with quality. Motor ability involves the following five areas: coordination, agility, speed, power, and balance.

Persons with good *cardiorespiratory endurance* are generally lean and physically active. They usually have a lot of energy. Cardiorespiratory endurance is defined as the ability of the body as a whole to take part in moderate activity for extended periods of time. If you have good cardiorespiratory endurance, then chances are good that you also have a strong heart, good blood vessels, and properly functioning lungs.

How Do I Become Physically Fit?

Everyone can become more physically fit. With some effort and determination you can begin to see and feel changes in yourself in just a couple of weeks once you begin a regular physical conditioning program. But before you start any exercise program, it's helpful to figure out your present physical condition. If you have diabetes, high blood pressure, asthma, a lot of headaches, or have recently broken any bones, you should see your doctor before beginning a training program. Generally it's a good idea to have a checkup, since your doctor can also tell you if there's any reason you shouldn't embark on a weight-reduction and/or exercise program.

Physical Fitness Status

To figure out how physically fit you are right now, you'll need to follow the six steps that are listed below. Be sure to record the results of each step in your log. At the very end of this chapter you'll see a sample Fitness Profile Worksheet that you might want to use in your log to record all this information. The six steps that you'll follow are:

STEP 1: Find out where you fall in comparison with the national averages in height and weight.
STEP 2: Figure out your percentage of body fat.
STEP 3: Figure out your level of heart and lung fitness.
STEP 4: Determine your body type.
STEP 5: Rate your feelings about yourself.
STEP 6: Pull together your diet and exercise needs.

STEP 1
Find out where you fall in comparison with the national averages in height and weight.

You probably have already recorded your height and weight in your log. If you haven't, do it now. Using the chart in Chapter 2, find out where you fall in comparison with the national averages in height and weight. Are you short, average, or tall in height? Are you light, average, or above average in weight?

Remember, averages are determined from a large group of people and are not necessarily ideal. Don't pass judgment on your physical fitness based only on your height and weight. When you've finished all six steps, then you'll be better able to figure out your present level of fitness.

STEP 2
Figure out your percentage of body fat.

The average female's body weight is about 26% fat. The average male's body weight is about 18% fat. These are average figures and aren't necessarily ideal. A certain amount of body fat is needed to help maintain body temperature at 98.6 degrees Fahrenheit (98.6°F) or 37 degrees Centigrade (37°C). Body fat is also needed to help protect many important internal organs such as the kidneys. Experts recommend that a healthy body weight for women and girls should aim for 20% to 25% body fat; for men and boys, the body weight should aim for 12% to 17% body fat. Body fat above 25% for women and 17% for men usually means that extra, unwanted weight is being carried around. The extra weight can be uncomfortable and may make the heart's job more difficult.

It's important to know that having less body fat than is recommended may be harmful. Athletes may have lower body fat percentages than those noted above but they get them by taking part in vigorous sports training programs. Although very low percentages of body fat may be healthy for athletes, they aren't recommended for most of us. With the right amount of exercise and good eating habits, you can stay within the recommended body fat percentages for your age and sex and like what you see in your mirror.

Here's a simple way you can estimate your body fat percentage. You'll be measuring the thickness of the fat underneath the back of your upper arm. You'll need a friend to help you. You'll also need a ruler and a pen. Be sure to record your results in your log.

Estimating Body Fat Percentage
1. Bend your left arm.
2. Have your friend measure the distance from the tip of your shoulder to the tip of your elbow. Then let your left arm fall relaxed at your side.
3. Find the halfway point and put a small mark there.
4. Now have your friend pinch your skin at the point marked using his or her left hand with the elbow held

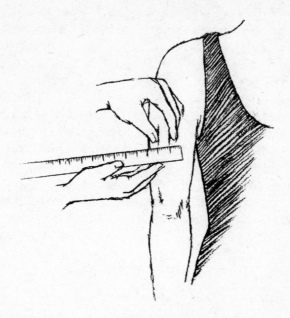

high. Try this a few times. Only the fatty tissue and skin, not the muscle, should be pinched (see drawing).

5. Have your friend measure the distance between his or her thumb and index finger, placing the ruler *below* the skinfold. Do *not* let the skinfold flatten. That would make the measurement larger.

6. Take two measurements. Then figure out the average.

$$\frac{\text{skinfold \#1} + \text{skinfold \#2}}{2} = \text{Average Skinfold}$$

7. Use the following tables to make a good guess at your percentage of body fat.

Girls'	Skinfold Thickness	1/4"	1/2"	3/4"	1"	1 1/4"
	% Body Fat	8%–13%	13%–18%	18%–23%	23%–28%	28%–33%
Boys'	Skinfold Thickness	1/4"	1/2"	3/4"	1"	1 1/4"
	% Body Fat	5%–9%	9%–13%	13%–18%	18%–22%	22%–27%

Do you fall within the recommended range of percentage of body fat? Usually, if you can pinch more than an inch of fat, you may need to be on a weight-loss program. But fat can be unevenly distributed over your body. So an upper arm measurement may not be the best picture of your total body fat. Remember, it's the whole picture that counts. Check with the mirror. Do you like what you see?

STEP 3
Figure out your level of heart and lung fitness.

You can get a fairly good idea of what your present level of cardiovascular fitness is by comparing your *resting heart rate* to others of your sex and age. It's easy to figure out your resting heart rate. You only have to take your pulse while you're resting comfortably. A stopwatch or a watch with a second hand is the only equipment you'll need.

Taking Your Pulse
1. Sit comfortably in a chair.
2. Using one hand, let your thumb rest on your chin. The other fingers of that hand should easily be able to feel a large artery at the side of the neck, the carotid artery. The artery will lie in front of the strip of

muscle running up and down the neck. Another pulse spot is located on your wrist, just below the base of your thumb. This is the radial pulse.

3. Check your watch or stopwatch and count the number of times the pulse beats in 1 minute. Do this 3 times and then take the average of all 3.
4. Compare your resting heart rate with those in your sex category on the chart below.

Women/Girls	Estimated Cardiovascular Level	Men/Boys
56–lower	very high	53–lower
64–57	high	60–54
71–65	moderate	65–61
79–72	low	76–66
above 80	very low	above 76

What is your estimated cardiovascular level? Record this information in your log.

STEP 4
Determine your body type.

Look in a full-length mirror or get a snapshot of you standing up. Compare your picture with the following body types called somatotypes:

The *ectomorph* is usually long and lean. Muscles appear long, and bones are long and delicate. The shoulders are generally narrow across and rounded, and the chest is relatively small.

The *endomorph* body type has hips that tend to be larger than the chest. The body seems stocky. All parts of the body are soft and round. The hands and feet are comparatively small.

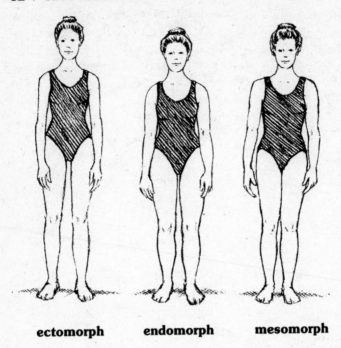

ectomorph   **endomorph**   **mesomorph**

The *mesomorph* body type has a chest that is more muscular and larger than the abdomen. The mesomorph seems to have an athletic build with a well-developed chest and smaller hips and waist. Muscles are developed and joints stand out.

You'll probably find that you are somewhere in-between, like an ectomesomorph, a leaner and more muscular type, or a mesoendomorph, a somewhat muscular yet rounder type.

None of the body types is right or wrong, better or worse. Your basic body type is determined in large part by what you inherited from your parents. You can shift closer to one type or another by exercising or not exercising and by gaining or losing weight.

STEP 5
Rate your feelings about yourself.

Sometimes a very good measure of your overall fitness is your mental attitude about yourself and your surroundings. Do you like yourself? Are you happy about the way you look? About the way you can contribute something to group activities? On a scale of 1 to 10, rate your self-image. Let 1 be low and 10 be high. Record this information in your log.

STEP 6
Pull together your diet and exercise needs.

One way to lose weight is to eat fewer calories. Another way is to exercise more and burn off some of those calories. Or you may choose to do a combination of eating less and increasing your exercise level.

In Chapter 4 you read about the seven steps to success that make up the LTTD Approach. Step 2, Adjusting Your Calorie Level, explained how to change the number of calories you eat each day to keep that calorie count in tune with your exercise level. In the five steps outlined below you'll have a chance to think about all the activities you do each day. Then you'll be able to estimate the number of calories you actually burn in a twenty-four-hour period.

1. Write down everything you do for two days. Then estimate the number of hours you spent each day in different kinds of activities. Use quarter hours if you can and account for 24 hours a day. To make it easier, include the time spent going between classes as class activity.

2. Use the chart included in this section to help you find the calories you used per pound in each activity that you've recorded. You'll see that the activities are in six categories ranging from almost no activity (sleeping) to very active exercise (running).

3. Then multiply the number of calories per pound per hour by the number of hours you have spent in that activity. For example, if you are 14 years old and slept 8 hours, 8 times 0.5 equals 4, the number of calories you used in sleeping per pound of body weight.

4. Next, add up the calories you used per pound in 24 hours.

5. Multiply this total by your weight to get an estimate of the calories used per day.

Do you remember Susan Smith from Chapter 3? She figured out that her ideal weight should be 120 pounds. Her first weight-reduction formula allowed her to eat 1200 calories a day and still lose weight. But when she did a rough adjustment of her calorie level to keep it in tune with her exercise level, she found that she could eat 1700 calories a day and still lose weight.

Susan has now decided to take a closer look at her actual daily activity level. She wants a better idea of how many calories she actually burns each day.

Form of Activity	*Sleeping*	*Sitting quietly* reading, writing, eating, sewing, watching TV, studying, attending class	*Light exercise* dressing, typing, playing piano, driving car, dishwashing, cooking, light laundry, light housework
Estimated calories per pound per hour at ages 10–18	0.5	0.9	1.2

Form of activity	*Moderate exercise*	*Active exercise*	*Very active exercise*
	bicycling, walking, active housework, or work like clerking which requires bending and stretching, babysitting when child is active, gym	dancing, skating, playing Ping-Pong, horseback riding	running, swimming, basketball, tennis
Estimated calories per pound per hour at ages 10–18	1.9	2.7	4.7

Susan's log for day 1 looks like this:

(light exercise)	6:30–7:00 AM dressing
(light exercise)	7:00–7:30 breakfast
(moderate exercise)	7:30–7:45 walking to school
(sitting quietly)	7:45 AM–2:30 PM classes in school
(moderate exercise)	(gym for 45 minutes)
(moderate exercise)	2:30–2:45 walking home
(light exercise)	2:45–3:15 eating snack
(sitting quietly)	3:15–4:00 studying
(very active exercise)	4:00–4:30 running
(very active exercise)	4:30–5:00 tennis
(light exercise)	5:00–5:30 shower
(light exercise)	5:30–6:00 dressing
(light exercise)	6:00–7:00 eating dinner
(light exercise)	7:00–7:30 cleaning up after dinner
(sitting quietly)	7:30–9:30 studying
(light exercise)	with 45 minutes of typing
(sleeping)	9:30 PM–6:30 AM sleeping

Next, Susan must figure out how many calories she used per pound in each activity. A quick and easy way to do this is to group together the activities she's done into the six categories listed in the activity chart.

sleeping category:	9 hours
sitting quietly category:	8 hours
light exercise category:	4 hours 45 minutes
moderate exercise category:	1 hour 15 minutes
active exercise category:	no time
very active exercise category:	1 hour

In the third step, Susan multiplies the number of calories per pound per hour by the number of hours she has spent in that activity. For Susan, step 3 would look like this:

sleeping category: 9 × 0.5 = 4.5 calories Susan burned per pound of her body weight while sleeping

sitting quietly category: 8 × 0.9 = 7.2 calories Susan burned per pound of her body weight

light exercise category: 4.75 × 1.2 = 5.7 calories Susan burned per pound of her body weight

moderate exercise category: 1.25 × 1.9 = 2.38 calories Susan burned per pound of her body weight

active exercise category: none

very active exercise category: 1 × 4.7 = 4.7 calories Susan burned per pound of her body weight

In the fourth step, Susan adds up the calories she used per pound in 24 hours. Step 4 looks like this:

$$4.5 + 7.2 + 5.7 + 2.38 + 4.7 = 22.48$$

In the last step, Susan multiplies the total she got in step 4 (22.48) by her weight (125 pounds) to get an estimate of the calories she burns per day.

$$22.48 \times 125 = 2810$$

According to this formula, Susan burns 2810 calories each day. This means that if Susan does burn 2810 calories each day, then she could eat that same amount to keep her weight the same. But if she wants to lose weight, she can either reduce her calorie intake or increase her exercise or do a little of both. If she followed a 1700 calorie diet, she would average about a two pound a week weight loss.

Try to figure out how many calories you burn each day. Keep track of your daily activities for at least two days so you'll get a more accurate picture of your daily activity level. Be sure to write down in your log the number of calories you burn each day.

Remember, the answer you get is a guide only and not a rigid one. However, this record will help you adjust the number of calories you get from food to the number of calories you use in various kinds of activity. Your weight and growth are good tests of how you balance the calorie supply and demand.

SAMPLE
FITNESS PROFILE WORKSHEET

Name: Date:

Height: Weight:

Step 1: I am in the _____ category in height and the _____ category in weight for my age and sex.

Step 2: skinfold #1 + skinfold #2 = sum
        sum ÷ 2 = average skinfold
        My approximate body fat percentage is:_____

Step 3: resting heart rate #1 + resting heart rate #2 + resting heart rate #3 = sum
        sum ÷ 3 = average resting heart rate
        My estimated cardiovascular level is:_____

Step 4: Right now, I most resemble an ectomorph?
                                    endomorph?
                                    mesomorph?

Step 5: At this moment, my self image is about:

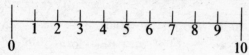

Step 6:
1. Log of daily activities:
2. Calories used per pound in each activity:
   sleeping category:_____
   sitting quietly category:_____
   light exercise category:_____
   moderate exercise category:_____
   active exercise category:_____
   very active exercise category:_____
3. Multiply number of calories per pound by number of hours spent in that activity:
   sleeping category:_____
   sitting quietly category:_____
   light exercise category:_____
   moderate exercise category:_____
   active exercise category:_____
   very active exercise category:_____
4. Add up calories used per pound in 24 hours:

   sleeping category + sitting quietly category + light exercise category + moderate exercise category + active exercise category + very active exercise category = total calories used per pound in 24 hours

5. Multiply total calories used per pound in 24 hours by your weight to get an estimate of the calories you burn each day:

   total calories used per pound in 24 hours × your weight = calories you burn each day

Your Goals and Expectations

You can develop your goals and expectations in a number of ways. First you must remember that your present level of fitness will determine your approach and what you need to improve. You should try to aim for a slow, steady level of increase in exercise and weight loss (if needed) instead of trying to undo in a few weeks what it may have taken you years to become. You should feel "pushed" after a workout, but you should never be gasping for air. If you're doing exercises in place or distance exercises to improve your cardiovascular fitness, you may find that your muscles and joints are slightly sore the next day. It should never be so bad that walking around or performing other activities becomes a real problem. Check the information in your log that you have outlined about your personal fitness needs. Then go on to Chapter 6 and get ready to begin your fitness program.

6

Fitness How-to's

By now you should have completed your physical assessment from Chapter 5. You're ready to make long-term changes in your exercise habits. Now you can design a program to better your overall fitness. To do this you'll want to include some type of regular cardiovascular exercise along with a series of muscle strength and endurance exercises.

Cardiovascular Fitness Program

Running, swimming, bicycling, roller-skating, cross-country skiing, dancing, and other similar continuous activities are aerobic. They all help to promote cardiovascular fitness. Aerobic exercise must be done at least three times a week with no more than two days between workouts or any gains you'll make in your cardiovascular fitness will begin to disappear. Whatever activity you choose must work you hard enough to keep a steady heart rate of about seventy percent to eighty percent of your maximal heart rate. That's why if you plan on using a team sport such as tennis as your aerobic exercise, you really must be a skilled player. Otherwise, the activity won't be continuous enough to help promote cardiovascular fitness.

So what's your maximal heart rate? By definition your maximal heart rate is the heart rate you would achieve if you were to run as fast as you could for as long as you could until you just had to stop to catch your breath. You can estimate your maximal heart rate by subtracting your age from 220. For example, a fourteen-year-old has an estimated maximal heart rate of 206 (220 − 14 = 206).

Once you've figured out your maximal heart rate, you'll want to figure out your target heart range (THR). You can do this by following these three steps:

Step 1: Find out your maximal heart rate (220 − your age = maximal heart rate)

Step 2: Multiply your maximal heart rate by 0.70 (maximal heart rate × 0.70)

Step 3: Multiply your maximal heart rate by 0.85 (maximal heart rate × 0.85)

Step 2 gives you the number of beats at the lower end of your target heart range and step 3 gives you the number of beats at the upper end of your target heart range. For example, a fourteen-year-old has a maximal heart rate of 206. When you multiply 206 by 0.70 as in step 2, you get 144.2. This is the number of beats at the lower end of the target heart range. In step 3, when you multiply 206 by 0.85, you get 175.1. This is the number of beats at the upper end of the target heart range. So a fourteen-year-old would have a target heart range of 144 to 175 beats per minute. It's important to figure out your own target heart range because it's within this range that your heart should beat while you're involved in your cardiovascular exercise.

Let's say you choose jogging as your cardiovascular exercise. Before you begin to jog, you should walk briskly for 2 to 5 minutes. This is your warm-up period. It's important to slowly ease yourself into whatever activity it is that you choose. Start out in slow motion for the first five minutes. This will help your body adjust to the load of work you'll soon be asking it to do. Your heart and lungs as well as your muscles need this time. Give it to them because without it they may give it to you! To prevent an injury before it happens, always warm up first.

Once you begin to jog, you should stop from time to time to check your heart rate. It should be beating somewhere within your target heart range. You already know how to take your pulse. Check back in Chapter 5 if you need to. But this time when you take your pulse, you should stop for just a moment and count the number of beats in 6 seconds instead of a full minute. Then multiply that number by 10. This will give you a good estimate of your heart rate for 60 seconds or 1 minute. For example, if your heart rate for 6 seconds is 15, you would multiply by 10 to get 150 as a working heart rate. If your target heart range is 144–175 beats per minute, then you know that you're exercising properly to help you improve your cardiovascular fitness.

In your log you might want to keep track of resting heart rates, heart rates after 5 minutes of exercising, after 10 minutes of exercising, at the end of your workout, and 2 minutes after you've stopped exercising. As time goes by, you should notice that your resting heart rate will slowly decrease and that your heart rate will return to the resting rate more quickly than when you first started. These are all good signs that your aerobic fitness is getting better.

Exercise Conditioning Program—Rules of the Road

Before you begin to design your own exercise conditioning program, there are some simple but very important rules you need to know.

RULE 1
Always warm up before you begin your conditioning program. If you're short on time, cut down on your conditioning exercises, not your warm-up. "Cold" muscles, those that haven't been warmed up, often are easily injured.

RULE 2
Stop an exercise if it hurts. A little stiffness or soreness in your muscles while doing an exercise and on the following day is normal. But a definite pain or ache in any joint or in your back or abdomen while doing an exercise is a signal to stop. Any exercise that causes you to strain unnecessarily should always be changed. There are plenty of exercises to choose from for each area of the body. Don't try to do too much, too soon, or too fast!

RULE 3
Before beginning an exercise, always be sure to do the pelvic tilt. You'll find a description of the pelvic tilt under

conditioning exercises. It's the first exercise in that section. By doing the pelvic tilt you flatten the lumbar curve in the lower part of your back. This will help to protect your back from too much strain.

RULE 4

When doing exercises that have you lie on your side, the standard form is resting on the underside of your upper arm with your hand supporting your head. Your free arm can then be used as a "kickstand" in front of you with your hand resting on the floor. This should keep you from rocking back and forth.

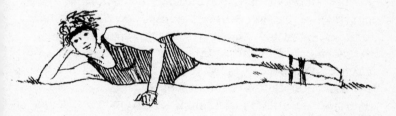

If you still feel shaky, you can bend your bottom leg for more support.

You should use this position for all exercises that state "Lie on your side" unless you're instructed differently.

RULE 5

Breathe normally. Sometimes you may find that you're holding your breath because you're concentrating so hard. But this only adds more stress to a stressful activity. The best advice is just to try to breathe as you do normally.

RULE 6

Don't bounce. Jerky, bouncing motions can lead to damaged muscles. Always move with control.

The exercises outlined in the conditioning program are divided into two major sections. The simple stretches described in section A are to be used for your warm-up. Always start with the warm-up exercises and do the stated number of repetitions for each stretch. Then choose two or three exercises for each area of the body from section B, the conditioning exercises. All of the exercises described in section B are grouped by the body area and muscles they work. Start the conditioning exercises with ten to twelve repetitions of each exercise.

Remember, if you're straining on an exercise, choose another one, at least for now. As you get stronger, you can always try the harder ones. You should aim for thirty repetitions of each exercise by adding on about five more repetitions each week. Try to do your exercise program two to three times a week. Try not to let more than two days sneak in between sessions.

You might want to try exercising with a friend. Maybe you might want to add music. Make your exercise time a fun time and you'll stick with it longer. Try to keep track of your program and progress by making a chart to put in your log. Be sure to record the exercises that you've chosen for each of the seven body parts, and the dates on which you've done your program. A sample chart is included at the end of this chapter.

Section A: Warm-Ups: Simple Stretches

1. Neck Roll

Stand with feet shoulder-width apart. Pelvic tilt. Arms at sides, tilt head over one shoulder trying to touch ear to shoulder. Roll head around to front, other side, and back. Return to starting position. Do all repetitions in one direction and then in the other. Do 10 times.

2. Shoulder Roll

Stand with feet shoulder-width apart. Pelvic tilt. Arms at sides, round shoulders forward, up, and then back, trying to press shoulder blades together. Return to starting position. Do all repetitions in one direction and then reverse directions, blades together first, then rounding forward. Do 10 times.

3. Arm Circle

Stand with feet shoulder-width apart. Pelvic tilt. Arms out to sides, shoulder level, make small circles. Complete 10 repetitions. Make medium circles. Complete 10 repetitions. Make large, controlled circles. Don't helicopter! Complete 10 repetitions. Repeat above in reverse direction.

4. Side Stretch

Stand with feet a bit wider than shoulder-width apart. Pelvic tilt. With one arm relaxed at side, the other one stretched overhead, slowly stretch to side of relaxed arm. Let arm stretch down side of leg. Keep head forward. Hold stretch for count of 10. Slowly return to upright position. Switch arm positions, bend to opposite side. Hold stretch for count of 10. Repeat stretches 2 to 3 more times to each side holding for count of 10. Increase the hold count instead of repetitions as you improve.

5. Heel Cord Stretch

Stand with one leg in front of the other. Keep feet parallel. Bend forward leg only as far as back leg's heel remains on the floor. Lean forward with torso and rest hands on knee or floor. Hold for count of 10. Repeat on other side. Do 2 to 3 times for each leg.

6. Hamstring (back of thigh) Stretch (A)

Start in position of heel cord stretch. Straighten front leg as much as possible while keeping heel of back foot flat on floor. Lean forward toward thigh of front leg. Hold for count of 10. Repeat with other leg. Do 2 to 3 times for each leg.

7. Hamstring/Heel Cord Stretch (B)

Start in hamstring stretch (A) position. Flex foot of forward leg as much as possible. Hold for count of 10. Repeat with other leg. Do 2 to 3 times for each leg.

8. Back and Hamstring Stretch

Stand with feet shoulder-width apart, arms at sides. Pelvic tilt. While continually keeping abdominals (stomach muscles) tight, _slowly_ lower torso to floor by curling down, leading with your head. Reach for the floor by your feet with your hands. Hold for count of 10. Slowly curl up. Repeat 3 times.

9. Quadricep (front of thigh) Stretch

Stand with one hand on desk top, table, or chair back for support. Pelvic tilt. With other hand grab ankle of same side and pull gently toward buttocks. Hold for count of 10. Repeat 3 times for each leg.

10. Jog in place, jump rope, or do jumping jacks for 2 to 3 minutes.

This will help increase the blood flow to the working muscles and ready you for exercise.

Section B: Conditioning Exercises

PELVIC TILT

Every time you are asked to take a standing position, unless otherwise stated, assume that you're to stand with your feet shoulder-width apart, arms resting comfortably at your sides. Straighten out the lumbar curve in your back by squeezing your buttocks' cheeks together while contracting your abdominal muscles. Do *not* try to suck your stomach in! If this is done, as soon as you try to breathe normally it will return to its original position!

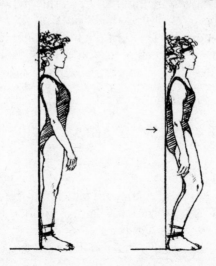

Try this. Walk over to a wall. Place your heels and back against the wall. You'll notice that your back does *not* lie flat against the wall. If you now tighten your buttocks (your knees may slightly flex) you should be able to feel the entire length of your back come in contact with the wall.

This happens because as you squeeze your buttocks tight, your pelvis (hips) actually tilts. That's why it's called the pelvic tilt.

The pelvic tilt should also be maintained in all exercises requiring you to lie flat on your back and in those in which you'll be raising or lowering all or some of your body weight, as in push-ups.

Again, simply squeeze your buttocks tight and the pelvic tilt should take place. When lying on the floor, you should be able to feel your back come into contact with the floor.

If you always remember to keep this pelvic tilt wherever possible, you'll find the results of exercising much more rewarding. The area of the body you intend to work will indeed be worked and you'll have a much lesser chance of developing lower back pain now and in the future.

FOR YOUR CHEST AND SHOULDERS

Chest Push-Ups

Begin on hands and knees. Place hands directly below shoulders, fingers turned in slightly. Tilt body forward so that most of your weight is over your hands; arms should be straight and knees on the floor. Pelvic tilt. (Back

should be straight.) Staying on your knees, lower yourself very slowly to the floor. When you reach the floor, relax briefly. Return to the starting position and repeat. To increase difficulty of exercise, push up as well as lowering to the floor without resting between repetitions. The difficulty of the exercise may again be increased by straightening your legs and raising up onto your toes instead of keeping your knees on the floor. Remember to make sure that your back remains flat throughout the exercise.

Hand Press

Sit or stand comfortably. Place palms together at chest level, elbows out to sides. Press palms together firmly for a slow count of 5, then relax. Be sure not to hold your breath. Try to breathe in when you're in the relaxed position and out when pressing palms together.

Partner Press

Sit facing a partner with arms extended in front of you at shoulder level. One of you should place your hands on the other's forearms, palms facing in. The other person should place his or her palms on your forearm facing out. Together, press against each other's forearms for a slow count of 5. Relax and repeat. When all of your repetitions are completed, switch positions and repeat.

Chest Toner

You'll need a pair of weights for this one. If you have none at home try using a 5-pound bag of coffee, or a 5-pound can of soup, or an old sock lined with a plastic bag filled with 5 to 10 pounds of sand or soil. Lie on your back with knees bent and feet flat on the floor. Pelvic tilt. Grip a weight at each side by your thighs. Breathe in and

raise the weights over your head almost to the floor. Exhale and return to your sides. Repeat.

FOR YOUR ARMS

Triceps (back of arms) Push-ups

Begin on hands and knees. Place hands directly below shoulders, fingers turned out slightly. Tilt body forward so that most of your weight is over your hands; arms should be straight and knees on the floor. Pelvic tilt. (Your back should be straight.) Remaining on knees, lower yourself very slowly to the floor, *keeping elbows tucked in close to the side of your body*. When you reach the floor, relax briefly. Return to the starting position and repeat.

To increase difficulty of the exercise, push up as well as lowering to the floor without resting between repeti-

tions. The difficulty of the exercise may again be increased by straightening your legs and raising up onto your toes, instead of keeping your knees on the floor. Remember to make sure that the curve of your back remains flat throughout the exercise.

Biceps Curl

You'll need a weight for this one. If you have none at home try using a 5-pound can of coffee, or a 5-pound can of soup, or an old sock lined with a plastic bag filled with 5 to 10 pounds of sand or soil. (For some exercises you will need 2 weights.) Stand with feet shoulder-width apart. Pelvic tilt. With weight in one hand, arm straight at your side and elbow tucked in close to your side near your hip, bring your hand and weight up toward your shoulder *without* moving your elbow away from the body. Return to starting position. Do all repetitions with one arm before repeating with the other.

Wall Push-away

Stand, facing a wall, hands on the wall about shoulder-width apart. Turn fingers out. Place feet out from wall about 20 inches. Pelvic tilt. Lean into the wall, bending your elbows so that they point toward the floor, *not* out to your sides. Straighten your arms and push away from the wall.

To make the exercise more difficult, move your feet farther away from the wall. **Be** sure to pelvic tilt.

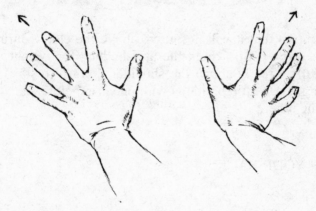

Triceps Press

Again, you'll need a weight for this one. Lie on your back with knees bent. Pelvic tilt. With weight in hand, place this hand by your ear, just above the shoulder. With other hand, hold the back of the arm with the

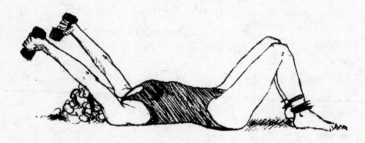

weight so that it will not move above the elbow during
the exercise. Straighten the arm holding the weight so
that it's directly above the shoulder. Return to starting
position. Do all repetitions with one arm before starting
on the other.

FOR YOUR BACK

The Weeder

Stand with feet shoulder-width apart. Bend from the
waist keeping back flat and abdominal muscles tight.
Remember to flex knees slightly. Let arms hang down
from your shoulders. Pull both arms straight back and
up, above the body as far as they will go. Return to the

starting position. Now pull them back, elbows high but forearms and hands still pointed toward the floor. Return to the starting position. This is one repetition.

Head and Arm Lift

Lie face down, knees bent, and cross feet in the air. With elbows bent, place one hand over the other, palms down, and rest your forehead on the back of your hands. Keeping thighs and knees on the floor, lift elbows first

and then your head and chest off of the ground. Do *not* jerk yourself up. Hold for a slow count of 5 and return to starting position. Repeat.

Pull-downs

You'll need a broom, mop, or any long pole for this one. Stand with feet shoulder-width apart. Pelvic tilt. Grasp pole with palms facing the floor, arms about shoulder-width apart. Inhale and lift the pole over the head and bend elbows as you pull the pole down behind the back, keeping it close to the body. Now extend the pole back up over the head and return to the original position. Always inhale each time you lift the pole overhead and exhale as you lower it.

FOR YOUR WAIST AND ABDOMEN

Curl-ups

Lie on floor with knees bent and feet in the air. Place hands on shoulders. Bring chin to chest and continue to "curl up" as much as you can *without* a jerky movement. Uncurl, returning to the original position. Repeat.

Reverse Curl

Assume the same starting position as for curl-ups, but place hands behind head, elbows resting on the ground. Try to contract your abdominal muscles while attempting

to bring your knees toward you as you *curl up*, starting with your buttocks. Do *not* throw your legs over your head! This is cheating! Keep your head and elbows on the ground. If this is difficult, hold on to the legs of a desk or chair with your hands and try the exercise this way.

Roll Overs

Lie on floor, arms out to sides shoulder level. Tuck knees into chest. Keeping arms flat, roll to one side and then to the other. Keep your knees as close to your chest as possible. This is one repetition. Repeat.

Side Bends

Stand with feet shoulder-width apart. Pelvic tilt. With arms at sides, bend to one side and then to the other. This is one repetition. Repeat.

To make exercise more difficult, place hands behind head, and later still, place arms overhead with fingers interlaced.

FOR YOUR HIPS AND BUTTOCKS

Buttock Lift

Lie on the floor with knees bent and feet flat on floor. With arms at sides, lift buttocks off the ground so that your body forms a straight line from neck to knees. Hold this for a count of 5. Return to starting position. Repeat.

On All Fours Side Leg Lift

On your hands and knees, straighten one leg out to the side. Raise and lower leg. Do all repetitions with this leg before repeating exercise with other side.

To increase difficulty, circle forward with straight leg without resting between repetitions.

Up 'n' Out, Up 'n' In

Lie facedown on floor with chin resting on the back of your hands. Keep legs straight. *Keeping your chin on your hands,* lift both legs up, part them in the air and lower them to the ground. Now, raise them back up, bring them back together and lower them. This is one repetition. *Note:* Do not perform this exercise if it bothers your back.

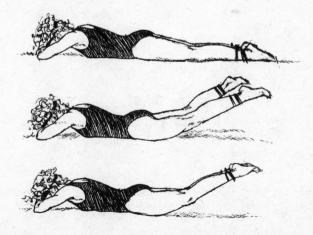

Side Leg Lift

Lie on your side with bottom leg bent for support. Lift the top leg so that when you look over your shoulder at it you are looking at its side, *not* at the front of its knee and thigh. You should feel this along the side of your hips and in your buttocks. Return to the starting position. Do all repetitions on this leg before repeating them on your opposite leg.

FOR YOUR THIGHS

Air Crosses

Lie on your back with your knees tucked into your chest and arms along sides. Your arms should be closely hugging the body. Hands should be tucked slightly under buttocks. Pelvic tilt. Straighten legs up toward the ceiling. Now, keeping back in contact with the floor, open legs wide, then bring them together, crossing them. Open them again, bring them together, and cross them in the opposite direction. Make sure you open and close legs with control. This is one repetition. Repeat.

Standing Kick

Stand, with the side of your body facing a chair **or** wall. Hold chair or wall for support. Pelvic tilt. Lift outside leg forward. Lower it. Now lift it to the side and lower it. Finally, lift it to the rear and lower it. Do *not* let your back arch. This is one repetition. Do all repetitions for one leg before repeating them with the other.

Knee to Nose

On hands and knees, tuck one knee up toward the chest. Now straighten this leg and lift the leg up to the rear. This is one repetition. Do all repetitions for one leg before repeating them with the other. If your back bothers you with this one, lift the leg only as high as your back.

Leg Lunge

Stand with feet together. Step forward with one leg and bend knee so that thigh is parallel with floor. Lean torso forward. Push back to starting position. Repeat with other leg. This is one repetition. *Do not* attempt this exercise if your knees bother you or if you are unable to keep your back from arching.

FOR YOUR LOWER LEG

Toe Raises

Stand with feet slightly apart, arms resting comfortably at your sides. Pelvic tilt. Bend knees only as far as you can keeping heels on the floor. Now, roll onto your toes. Push up to straighten your legs and then return to your heels and the starting position. This is one repetition. Repeat.

Toe Ups

Sit on a table or desk so that your feet do *not* touch the floor. Let your toes drop toward the floor naturally. Now flex your feet so that your toes approach your calves. Hold for a count of 5 and relax. Repeat.

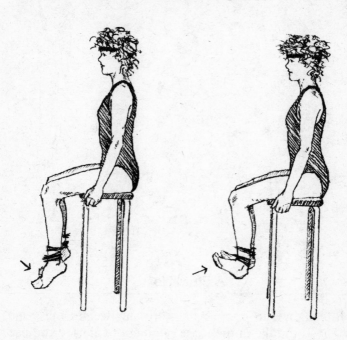

Drop Ups

Stand on the bottom of a set of stairs. Hold the railings or wall for support. Ease off the stairs so that only the balls of your feet and toes remain on the stairs. Let your heels slowly drop as far as they will. (You'll feel a stretch up the back of your calves.) Now, raise up onto your toes. Repeat.

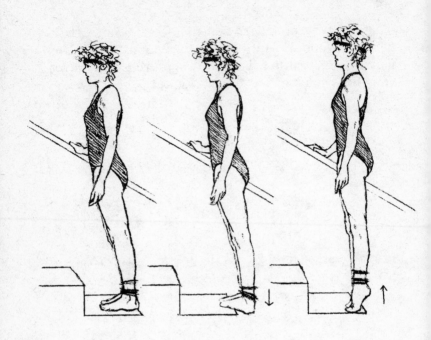

A Final Note

Remember, to be able to keep your weight the same you need to take in the same number of calories you use up by exercising, sleeping, and doing light activities. Every move you make uses calories.

Would you like to lose one pound? You'll need to leave out by dieting or use up by exercising up to about 3500 calories. You can get rid of the 3500 calories by combining dieting and exercising. You may want to refer to the calorie count for common activities to help you plan your diet and exercise program.

CALORIE COUNT FOR COMMON ACTIVITIES

Activity	*Calories burned per hour*
walking slowly	170
walking fast	350
jogging	450
biking	500
swimming	685
running	900

CALORIE COUNT FOR OTHER ACTIVITIES

Activity	*Calories burned per hour*
sleeping	60
tennis, singles	410
mountain climbing	600
skiing, downhill, 10 mph	600
skiing, cross-country	1150

SAMPLE EXERCISE PROGRAM

Name:

Exercises	*Dates*							
Warm-ups								
Neck Roll								
Shoulder Roll								
Arm Circle								
Side Stretch								
Heel Cord Stretch								
Hamstring (back of thigh) Stretch								
Hamstring/Heel Cord Stretch								
Back and Hamstring Stretch								
Quadriceps (front of thigh) Stretch								
Jog in Place, Jump-Rope, or Jumping Jacks								

Exercises	*Dates*								
Major Areas Chest and Shoulders									
Arms									
Back									
Waist and Abdomen									
Hips and Buttocks									
Thighs									
Lower Leg									

7

The New You

Congratulations! You're on your way. The new lean you will be happier and healthier than before. This is the beginning of a lifetime of proper diet and exercise. You'll look and feel wonderful.

Can you stay this way? The answer is yes, but you may not! Your family and friends, and most importantly you, can be your best helpmates or your biggest obstacle in your effort to remain lean and fit. Here's what to do to gather those forces and make them work for you!

Family

You may want your family to do some of the following things to help. It's very important that you tell them these things. You can't expect them to already know what you want them to do. Your family probably wants to help you, so don't be afraid to tell them what you need.

It might be helpful if you asked your family to *keep certain foods out of the house or out of your easy reach.*

Here are some things you might want to say: "Can we keep food behind the cupboard doors? When the food sits out on top of the refrigerator and on the counters, I find it hard to resist." Or you might try, "Please don't buy any more cookies for me; but if you want to buy them, get the kinds I don't really like. When I want cookies, or ice cream, I can buy them at the store a little at a time instead of having a house full of those temptations."

You might also want to ask your family to *keep certain foods more available*. Tell them, "When you go to the store, please buy more fresh carrots, a few diet salad dressings, and some extra fruit. It helps me when these things are there after school for quick snacks instead of cookies and soda."

Sometimes you might want your family to *keep your diet a family secret*. Say, "I'm more successful when others don't know, and then nag me, about my diet. I'd like it if we didn't tell anyone right now and then later we could surprise them."

You also might want to ask that your *foods be cooked differently*. "Instead of putting the butter on the potatoes and vegetables could you please serve them plain so we can put our own on if we want?" Ask for more baked and broiled foods rather than ones that are fried. Perhaps you may say, "I'm eating less now, so you can cook less and then not have to be worried about leftovers. I'm just as pleased with fruit for dessert. Try it. I won't complain."

If you *serve yourself* you can take just the amount of food you'd like to eat. Say, "Please let me dish out the amount of food I know I need instead of you serving me. My goal is to serve myself about half of what I need the first time around. Then if I'm still hungry, I'll go back for the other half during seconds."

Ask your family to *stop nagging*. "Please let me be the one to bring up the subject of my weight. It's a touchy subject. I know you may mean well, but being nagged doesn't help me. In fact, it irritates me even more. Sometimes it makes me eat just because I'm so angry."

Your family should *start noticing and commenting on the positive things*. "If you really want to help me keep my weight under control, you can start by ignoring me when you see me doing what I shouldn't since I know very well when I'm going off my diet. Instead, give me a few good words when you see me making some positive changes. For example, give me a pat on the back if you see me cut down on butter and gravy so I can work in a small piece of your chocolate cake."

Tell your family to *stop giving you food gifts*. "Instead of giving me a box of candy or baking my favorite dessert at special times, I would really like a new outfit or a new album. Please show me your love in a non-food way. I won't think you don't love me anymore if you stop giving me food treats!"

Your family should *stop offering you food*. You might tell them, "I promise that if I want some food or if I'm hungry, I'll ask. Meanwhile, please don't ask me if I want a second helping."

See how comfortable you feel with some of the above examples of how to talk to your family. Practice in your own words a few times before you really talk to them. If you're more of a quiet or silent type, write them a note with some of your ideas. No matter which way you choose, tell them!

To help get you started, plan a date for telling your family and write it down on a piece of paper or in your diet notebook. Under the date list three ways you want your family to help you.

Friends

Has this ever happened to you? You're with a friend and you pass by an ice cream store and your friend says:

FRIEND: "I'll have one if you do."

YOU: "I don't think I should."

FRIEND: "Oh come on. It can't hurt just this once."

YOU: "No. I've been trying hard to watch my weight and I don't want to undo my hard work."

FRIEND: "Well then, you've been so good you deserve to treat yourself. Besides, we'll be walking home and you can burn it off. And they have my favorite flavor."

YOU: "Well . . ."

Now you could end up with 350 or more extra calories and feel guilty too. Because you don't want your family to know you "cheated," you'll probably eat your full dinner at home so no one suspects you. Then you'll really feel like you've blown it and give up and feel bad that you've failed.

If you want to avoid this kind of outcome, you need to learn to be more assertive. You're the one who has trained your friend to know that if you are asked enough, you always give in. To counteract this obstacle, you have to train your friend in a new way. Be ready for friends to act a bit surprised at the new you. They may test your strength at sticking to your guns. If you are asked six times, be ready to say, *"NO THANKS,"* seven times.

Here's how you might change the first scene. Instead of saying "okay," try one of these endings.

1. "No, no, no, a thousand times no. If you ask me again I'll still say no." Such repetition gets across the idea that you really mean it. If your friend hears you stall or say "well," you will seem to be weakening.
2. "Let's keep walking. If we still want some we'll come back for it."
3. "I'll wait here while you go and get yours. I don't want any today."

Do you have a friend like the one in the example? If so are you willing to change what you say to this person? What will you say? How will you say, "No thank you," next time? Write your ideas down on a piece of paper or in your diet notebook.

Eating Out

Eating in a restaurant or a school cafeteria can be a difficult time for you when you're on a diet. Here are some tips to make it over this hurdle.

TIP 1: Check out the menu before going through the line or before you order. Decide how you want to spend your calories. For example, if they're having one of your favorite desserts, skip the fries and get the dessert.

TIP 2: Look for the main dishes that are baked or broiled instead of fried.

TIP 3: Ask them to leave out the gravy or sauce.

TIP 4: Order the salad dressing on the side so you can control how much to put on. Ask if they have diet dressing or oil and vinegar. (Helpful hint: oil has calories, but vinegar doesn't.)

TIP 5: Ask the server not to bring a basket of rolls. If they're already there, put them at the other end of the table.

TIP 6: Leave some food behind. The greater personal waste comes if you put more food inside you than you need.

TIP 7: Instead of a sandwich, get the filling on a salad or a separate plate. You may want to eat just half the bread.

You

Learn to reward yourself! It will help you with your dieting and with many other things in your life. Rewarding yourself is really a skill and an art. You need to perfect it and make it work for you.

Often the rewards an overweight person chooses aren't helpful. For example: Rebecca promised herself she'd get a new haircut if she got her weight under control. Meanwhile she felt messed-up and unattractive in her old hair style. Holding off on her haircut ended up making her feel defeated. As a result, Rebecca didn't lose much weight. She'd have been better off to start out her weight loss plans with a new haircut that made her feel good about herself.

Here are some tips to help you learn how to reward yourself. Go on and be good to you!

TIP 1: Be nice to yourself *now*. Don't wait until you're thin. You need pampering right now! If you do things for yourself that make you feel good, it will be easier to stick to your new lower calorie habits.

TIP 2: Have at least one pair of jeans and one nice outfit that fit you now. In order to feel good about yourself, you need to feel you look good and not like an overstuffed duffle bag. As you lose weight, get clothes to fit the new you. You don't need a whole new wardrobe. Get something that makes you feel good. Baggy clothes can make you feel just as bad as ones that are too tight.

TIP 3: Treat yourself to a bunch of flowers, some new makeup, or a new album—whatever makes you happy.

TIP 4: Spend your allowance on something you really want. You *deserve* it.

TIP 5: Buy something you really want for yourself and gift-wrap it. Put it in your locker or in your room as a good reminder. When you reach a small goal, open it!

Learn to use your imagination to help you control your eating habits. If you think you'll fail, you probably will. For example: If you're going out with friends and before you go you say to yourself, "I just know I'm going to overeat at the restaurant," you're really *planning* or setting yourself up to fail. Instead, imagine some of the following mind games.

GAME 1: Picture yourself at a party. Mentally practice the whole scene. Who is there? What kind of food is around? How is it served? Pretend the hostess is offering you some chips, dip, and coke. But you've seen the brownies and would really rather save the calories for them. Imagine saying, "No thank you. I'm not hungry yet. The brownies look great. I'll have one of those in a bit."

GAME 2: You can change a sour or bad mood by using your imagination. Think about a favorite place. Maybe you like the beach, the mountains, or being in a special room. It should be a place where you can be comfortable and at peace. Fill in all the details in your mind. What's the temperature? Is there a breeze? Are birds chirping? Mentally go there to relax alone.

GAME 3: Daydream about going to a department store and looking in the windows at an outfit you'd love to wear. Imagine going inside to a rack with the smaller sizes and trying on the outfit you like. It fits just right!

GAME 4: Visualize yourself as the guest of honor at an awards ceremony. As you listen you can hear all the good things everyone is saying about you.

GAME 5: Go back in time. Remember something nice that happened to you. Relive those feelings that made you feel great.

You've worked hard to get your weight under control. You're lean and trim and feel physically fit. Go with those good feelings and make them work for you. Good luck!

Glossary

Aerobic Requiring that oxygen be present, such as exercise performed over a long period of time.

Anorexia nervosa A medical condition associated with extreme body-weight loss and generally a very distorted body image.

Baseline information Data gathered before the start of a new program which is used to watch progress or change over time.

Bulimarexia, bulimea A medical condition usually associated with normal body weight and the practice of eating food and purging (vomiting) and/or the overuse of laxatives to maintain weight.

Calorie A measure of energy contained in food or used up during work, exercise, sleeping, and other bodily processes such as breathing and pumping blood.

Cardiorespiratory fitness The ability of the body to pump blood, oxygen, and nutrients to the muscles in order to work/exercise for longer periods of time.

Cardiovascular Relating to the heart and blood system of the body.

Chronological age Age in years determined by the sequence or order of years; example: a fifteen-year-old is chronologically older than a thirteen-year-old.

Conditioning exercises Those exercises which help muscles to develop tone.

Diet pills Medications, often of amphetamine or dexedrine origin, which are used to lower appetite during a weight loss program or activity.

Dextrose The simple sugar found in starch. Also called glucose.

Dehydration The excessive loss of fluid.

Ectomorph Body type characterized by slender, long, lean body parts (such as arms and legs).

Endomorph Body type characterized by soft, round, and full body parts (such as arms and legs).

Fructose The simple sugar found in fruits.

Genetic Relating to heredity, the tendency for characteristics to occur because parents have them; example: parents with blue eyes having children with blue eyes.

Growth pattern The pattern of increase in body height, weight, and/or head circumference over time.

Heart rate The number of heartbeats per minute.

Kilogram 1000 grams; the equivalent of 2.2 pounds.

Laxatives Medications that cause a loosening or softening of the stool to relieve constipation and permit bowel elimination.

Malnutrition A state of nutritional imbalance.

Maximum growth age or rapid growth phase The period of time in which a fast increase occurs in height and possibly weight that generally comes before or at the same time as the beginning of puberty.

Menstrual flow The normal and regulated discharging of blood, fluids, and tissue from the uterus in non-pregnant females, also called the period.

Mineral An essential nutrient element needed in very small amounts to help with normal body processes.

Mesomorph Body type characterized by muscular, firm, strong body parts (such as arms and legs).

Muscle endurance The capability of muscles to perform work or exercise over long time periods.

Muscle fibers Proteins that make up muscle tissue.

Nutrient An ingredient naturally occurring in or added to foods which provides nourishment for the growth and repair of body tissues. Nutrients include vitamins, minerals, protein, carbohydrates, and lipids (fats).

Nutritionist A person who has advanced training in nutrition science and a professional registration in dietetics (registered dietitian or R.D.) from the American Dietetic Association.

Puberty The period of time of becoming able to reproduce sexually, marked by the development of sex organs and secondary sex characteristics such as facial and armpit hair and the beginning of menstruation in females.

Protein A nutrient containing nitrogen that is needed for the normal growth and repair of body tissue and other key processes.

Polyunsaturated fat Vegetable fats that are generally more liquid or softer in nature, such as oils or soft margarine; associated with a lower risk of heart disease.

Saturated fat Animal fat or hardened vegetable fat, associated with greater risk of heart disease.

Secondary sex characteristics Armpit and facial hair and development of testicles in males and armpit hair and breast enlargement in females.

Sperm, Spermatozoa   The motile cells produced by males which are capable of fertilizing the female egg.

Strengthening exercises   Those exercises which cause muscles to do more work.

Sucrose   Simple table sugar.

Vitamin   A nutrient present usually in small amounts in man or foods that are needed for life.

Warm-up exercises   Those exercises that allow muscles to get longer or to get ready for more difficult exercises without feeling uncomfortable.

For Further Reading

Berland, Theodore and The Editors of Consumer Guide. *Rating the Diets*. A Signet Book. Skokie, Illinois: Publications International, Ltd., 1979.

Deutsch, Ronald. *The New Nuts Among The Berries: How Nutrition Nonsense Captured America*. Palo Alto, California: Bull Publishing, 1977.

Katch, Frank, and William McArdle. *Nutrition, Weight Control and Exercise*. Second edition. Boston: Houghton Mifflin Co., 1977.

National Academy of Sciences. *Conference on Adolescent Behavior and Health*. Summary. Washington, D.C.: IOM Publications, No. 78-004, October 1978.

Science and Education Administration, U.S. Department of Agriculture. *Food: The Hassle-free Guide to a Better Diet*. Home and Garden Bulletin No. 228 (no date).

Appendix

THE VITAMIN AND MINERAL CONTENT OF COMMON FOODS

Food	Amount	Vitamin A International Units	Ascorbic Acid Vitamin C
Milk, whole	1 cup	310	2 mg.
Milk, low fat	1 cup	500	2
Milk, skim fortified	1 cup	500	2
Cheddar cheese	1 ounce	300	0
Yogurt, low fat	1 cup	150	2
Cottage cheese	½ cup	185	trace
Apricot			
regular	1	965	3.5
dried	½ cup	7085	8
Cantaloupe	½	9240	90
Peach	1	1330	7
Tangerine	1	360	27
Watermelon	1 slice	2510	30
Orange	1	260	66
Papaya	1	2450	78
Mango (100 gm)	1	4800	35
Strawberries	½ cup	45	44
Prune Juice	1 cup	—	5.0
Asparagus	½ cup	655	19
Green Beans	½ cup	340	7.5
Broccoli	1 spear	4500	162
Brussels sprouts	½ cup	405	67
Carrots	½ cup	8140	4.5
Lettuce, leaf	½ cup	525	5
Peas	½ cup	585	7
Spinach, raw	½ cup	2230	14

Thiamin *Vitamin B_1*	*Riboflavin* *Vitamin B_2*	*Niacin*	*Calcium*	*Iron*
0.09 mg.	0.4 mg.	0.2 mg.	291 mg.	0.1 mg.
0.1	0.4	0.2	297	0.1
0.09	0.37	0.2	302	0.1
0.01	0.11	trace	204	0.2
0.1	0.49	0.3	415	0.2
0.002	0.18	0.15	67.5	0.15
0.01	0.13	0.2	6	0.16
.005	0.1	2.1	43	3.6
.11	0.08	1.6	38	1.1
0.02	0.05	1.0	9	0.5
0.05	0.02	0.1	34	0.3
0.13	0.13	0.9	30	2.1
0.13	0.05	0.5	54	0.5
0.06	0.06	0.4	28	0.4
0.05	0.05	1.1	10	0.4
0.02	0.05	0.45	15	0.75
0.03	0.03	1.0	36	1.8
0.11	0.13	1.0	15	0.45
0.05	0.05	0.3	23	0.4
0.16	0.36	1.4	112	1.4
0.06	0.11	0.6	25	0.8
0.04	0.04	0.4	25	0.45
0.01	0.02	0.1	7	0.4
.07	0.05	0.7	22	1.6
.03	0.05	0.15	25	0.8

Food	Amount	Vitamin A International Units	Ascorbic Acid Vitamin C
Squash			
winter	½ cup	4805	13
summer	½ cup	410	10
Sweet Potato,			
mashed	½ cup	9940	13
Tomato	½ cup	1035	20
regular	1	1110	28
juice	1 cup	1940	39
Fresh Greens:			
Collard	1 cup	14,820	144
Kale	1 cup	9130	102
Mustard	1 cup	8120	67
Turnips	1 cup	8270	68
Dried Beans,			
Peas	½ cup	—	—
Liver	3 ounces	45,390	23
Pork, Ham	3 ounces	—	—
Beef	3 ounces	50	—
Lamb	3 ounces	—	—
Veal	3 ounces	—	—
Sardines in			
oil	3 ounces	190	—
Salmon with			
bones	½ cup	80	—
Peanuts	1 ounce	—	—
Fortified Wheat			
Cereal	½ cup	705	5.5

Thiamin Vitamin B₁	*Riboflavin Vitamin B₂*	*Niacin*	*Calcium*	*Iron*
0.05	0.13	0.7	26	0.8
0.05	0.08	0.8	26	0.4
0.06	0.05	0.7	32	1.
0.06	0.035	0.8	7	0.6
0.07	0.05	0.9	16	0.6
0.12	0.07	1.9	17	2.2
0.21	0.38	2.3	357	1.5
0.11	0.2	1.8	206	1.8
0.11	0.2	0.8	193	2.5
0.15	0.33	0.7	252	1.5
0.25	0.13	1.3	90	4.9
0.22	3.56	14	9	7.5
0.40	0.15	3.1	8	2.2
.05	0.15	4.0	9	2.5
.15	0.23	4.7	0.6	1.4
0.06	0.21	4.6	9	2.7
0.02	0.17	4.6	372	2.5
0.04	0.21	9	223	0.9
0.05	0.02	3.1	11.5	0.37
0.17	0.21	1.7	6	41.5

THE VITAMIN AND MINERAL CONTENT OF FAST FOODS

	Vitamin A International Units	Ascorbic Acid Vitamin C
Arby's		
Roast Beef	—	—
Junior Roast Beef	—	—
Turkey Deluxe	—	—
Dairy Queen		
Cone, small	100	—
Cone, regular	300	—
Dip Cone, small	100	—
Dip Cone, regular	300	—
Banana Split	750	18 mg.
Brazier Fries, small	trace	3.6
McDonald's		
Egg McMuffin	97	1.4
Big Mac	530	2.2
Cheeseburger	345	1.6
Hamburger	82	1.7
Quarter Pounder	133	—
Quarter Pounder w/cheese	660	2.7
Filet-O-Fish	42	1.4
Regular Fries	17	12.5
Taco Bell		
Bean Burrito	1657	15.2
Enchirito	1178	9.5
Taco	120	0.2
Tostada	3152	9.7
Wendy's		
Single Hamburger	94	0.6
Double Hamburger	128	1.5
Single w/cheese	221	0.7
Double w/cheese	439	2.3
Chili	1188	2.9
French Fries	40	6.4

Thiamin Vitamin B₁	Riboflavin Vitamin B₂	Niacin	Calcium	Iron
0.30 mg.	0.34 mg.	5 mg.	80 mg.	3.6 mg.
0.15	0.17	3	40	1.8
0.45	0.34	8	80	2.7
0.03	0.14	—	100	—
0.09	0.26	—	200	—
0.03	0.17	—	100	—
0.09	0.34	—	200	0.4
0.60	0.60	0.8	350	1.8
0.06	trace	0.8	trace	0.4
0.47	0.44	3.8	226	2.9
0.39	0.37	6.5	157	4.0
0.25	0.23	3.8	132	2.4
0.25	0.18	4.0	51	2.3
0.32	0.28	6.5	63	4.1
0.31	0.37	7.4	219	4.3
0.26	0.20	2.6	93	1.7
0.12	0.02	2.3	9	0.6
0.37	0.22	2.2	98	2.8
0.31	0.37	4.7	259	3.8
0.09	0.16	2.9	120	2.5
0.18	0.15	0.8	191	2.3
0.24	0.36	5.8	84	5.3
0.43	0.54	10.6	138	8.2
0.38	0.43	6.3	228	5.4
0.49	0.75	11.4	177	10.2
0.22	0.25	3.4	83	4.4
0.14	0.07	3.0	16	1.2

TRADEOFFS YOU MAY WANT TO MAKE

TRADE VALUE FOR SNACK FOODS

Snack Food

R. T. FRENCH: Frozen Pizza Little Sausage, Cheese and Pepperoni

Tiny Cocktail Weiners

Tiny Vienna Sausages

Triscuits

Sociables

Party rye bread

Popcorn (commercial)

NABISCO: Bacon-flavored thin cracker

Sesame Snack crackers

Cheese Tid-Bits

Wheat Thins

Ritz Crackers

Melba Toast Rounds

FRITO-LAY: Fritos, Regular, Bar-B-Q

DORITOS: Regular, Nacho Cheese, Cheese, Taco

LAY'S: Potato Chips, Sour Cream & Onion, Bar-B-Q, Ruffles

FRITO-LAY: Pretzels

VERI-THIN: Pretzels

SOFT DRINKS: Mineral Water and diet sugar-free carbonated beverages are
all "freebies"—no nutritive value.

Amount	*Calories*	*Trades*
1 pizza	160	1½ breads, 1 fat
3	100	1 high-fat meat
3	100	1 high-fat meat
7 wafers	147	1½ breads, 1 fat
14 crackers	126	1 bread, 1 fat
4 slices	70	1 bread
3 cups	123	1 bread, 1 fat
14	150	1 bread, 1¾ fats
9	135	1 bread, 1½ fats
32	172	1 bread, 2 fats
16	144	1½ breads, 1 fat
7	126	1 bread, 1 fat
8	70	1 bread
1 ounce	150	1 bread, 1¾ fats
1 ounce	140	1 bread, 1½ fats
1 ounce	153	1 bread, 1¾ fats
1 ounce	110	1½ breads
1 ounce	100	1 bread, ½ fat

TRADE VALUE FOR FAST FOODS

	Approximate Calories	*Approximate Trade*
Arby's		
Junior Burger	220	1½ meats, 2 breads
Turkey Deluxe	510	3 meats, 3 breads, 3 oils/fats
Roast Beef	350	3 meats, 3 breads, 1 fat
Junior Roast Beef	220	1½ meats, 2 breads
Burger King		
Whopper	606	3½ meats, 4 breads, 3 oils/fats
Whopper junior	285	1 meat, 2 breads, 2 oils/fats
Hamburger	252	1 meat, 2 breads, 1 oil/fat
Cheeseburger	305	2 meats, 2 breads, 1 oil/fat
Hot Dog	291	1½ meats, 2 breads, 1 oil/fat
French Fries (Regular)	214	1½ breads, 2½ fats
Dairy Queen		
Small cone	110	1 milk, ½ bread
Medium cone	230	2 milks, 1 bread
Small dipped cone	150	1 milk, 1 bread
Medium dipped cone	300	2 milks, 2 breads
Small sundae	170	1 milk, 2 oils/fats
Medium sundae	300	2 milks, 3 oils/fats
Banana split	540	2 fruits, 4 milks, 3 oils/fats
Hot fudge brownie delight	580	1 bread, 4 milks, 4 oils/fats
Brazier Burger	260	1 meat, 2 breads, 1 fat
Brazier Cheeseburger	318	2 meats, 2 breads, 1 fat
French Fries	200	1½ breads, 2 oils/fats
Dunkin Donut		
Plain Donut	240	2 breads, 2 oils/fats
Honey Dipped Donut	260	2½ breads, 2 oils/fats
Chocolate Donut	240	2 breads, 2 oils/fats
Howard Johnson's		
Small dish ice cream—vanilla, ½ cup	210	1 milk, 1 bread, 1 oil/fat
Small dish Sherbet—½ cup	132	2 breads
Fried Clams, 5 ounces	395	2½ meats, 2 breads, 3 oils/fats

	Approximate Calories	*Approximate Trade*
McDonald's		
Egg McMuffin	352	2 meats, 2½ breads, 1 fat
French Fries (small)	211	2 breads, 1½ fats
Hamburger	257	1 meat, 2 breads, 1 oil/fat
Cheeseburger	306	2 meats, 2 breads, 1 oil/fat
Quarter Pounder	418	3 meats, 2 breads, 1½ oils/fats
Quarter Pounder with cheese	518	4 meats, 3 breads, 2 oils/fats
Big Mac	541	3 meats, 3½ breads, 3 oils/fats
Filet-O-Fish	402	3 meats, 2 breads, 2 oils/fats
Pizza Hut		
Individual Cheese Pizza (thin crust)	1000	3 meats, 12 breads
½, 10″ Thin Crust Beef Pizza	490	2½ meats, 5 breads
½, 10″ Thin Crust Cheese Pizza	450	2 meats, 4½ breads
½, 10″ Thin Crust Pepperoni Pizza	430	2½ meats, 4½ breads
½, 10″ Thin Crust Supreme Pizza	510	2½ meats, 4½ breads, 1 vegetable
Taco Bell		
Taco	186	1 meat, 1 bread, 1 vegetable
Tostada	179	1½ meats, 1½ breads, 1 vegetable
Bean Burrito	343	2½ starchy vegetables, 2 breads, 1 vegetable
Frijole	230	2 starchy vegetables, 1½ breads
Enchirito	454	2½ starchy vegetables, 2½ breads, 1 vegetable

Note to Teens: These foods are generally quite high in animal fat. While the trade values have been listed and include some oil/fat and meat equivalents, your diet should have more vegetable oils and lower fat animal products than a totally fast food diet would have.

APPROXIMATE CALORIC VALUES OF COMMON FOODS

	Calories
Beverages	
Carbonated, 8 ounces:	
Cola	95
Ginger ale	75
Lemonade	110
Coffee, black, 1 cup	5
Milk type:	
Cocoa with milk, 8 ounces	245
Eggnog, 8 ounces	290
Ice cream soda, 1	260
Malted milkshake, chocolate, 8 ounces	500
Milk, 8 ounces:	
Buttermilk, skim	90
Evaporated	345
Skim	90
Whole	160
Milkshake, chocolate, 8 ounces	420
Tea, 1 cup	2
Breads and Cereal Products	
Bagel	165
Biscuit, 2″ diameter	100
Breads, 1 slice:	
Boston brown, 3″ × ¾″	100
Raisin	65
Rye	60
White	65
Whole Wheat	65
Cereals:	
Cooked, ½ cup:	
Cornmeal	60
Farina	50
Oatmeal	65
Dry:	
Bran flakes, 1 cup	105

	Calories
Corn flakes, 1 cup	100
Puffed rice, 1 cup	60
Puffed wheat, 1 cup	55
Wheat flakes, 1 cup	105
Wheat, shredded, 1 biscuit	90
Cornbread, 2″ square	110
Crackers:	
Graham, 2½″ square	30
Saltine, 2″ square	15
Flour, all-purpose, 1 tablespoon	30
Macaroni, cooked, ½ cup	95
Muffin, 3″ diameter	120
Noodles, cooked, ½ cup	100
Pancake, 4″ diameter	60
Popover, 1 average	110
Rice, cooked, ½ cup	115
Rolls, 1 average:	
Frankfurter	120
Hamburger	120
Hard	155
Pan, 1 ounce	85
Sweet	180
Spaghetti, cooked, ½ cup	80
Tortilla, 6″ diameter	65
Waffle, 7″ diameter	210
Wheat germ, 3 tablespoons	100
Zwieback, 1 piece	30

Cheese

American, 1 ounce	105
Cheddar, 1 ounce	115
Cottage, ¼ cup	60
Cream, 1 ounce	105
Parmesan, 1 ounce	130
Spread, 1 ounce	80
Swiss, 1 ounce	105

Desserts

Apple Betty, ½ cup	210
Brownies, 2″ square	145

	Calories
Cake:	
Angel food, 10″ diameter, 1/12	135
Chocolate, chocolate icing, 2 layer, 1/16	235
Cupcake, plain, 2½″ diameter	90
Fruit, 8″ loaf, 1/30	55
Pound, ½″ slice	140
Sponge, 10″ diameter, 1/12	195
White, chocolate icing, 2 layer, 1/16	250
Cookies:	
Fig Bar, 1	56
Chocolate chip	50
Ginger snap	20
Oatmeal with raisins, 3″ diameter	65
Sandwich	50
Shortbread	35
Sugar, 3″ diameter	90
Vanilla wafer	15
Custard, ½ cup	150
Meats *(3 ounces cooked)*	
Chuck	180
Corned Beef	185
Hamburger	185
Liver, fried	195
Roast:	
Rib	210
Rump	180
Steak:	
Flank	170
Porterhouse	190
Round	165
Sirloin	175
T-Bone	190
Lamb:	
Chop, loin	160
Roast:	
Leg	160
Shoulder	175
Pork:	
Chop, loin	230

	Calories
Ham:	
Cured	160
Fresh	185
Roast, loin	215
Tenderloin	205
Veal:	
Chop, loin	175
Cutlet	185
Roast	145
Miscellaneous:	
Bacon, 2 medium slices	90
Bologna, 3" × 1/8" slice	80
Braunschweiger, 2" × 1/4" slice	65
Deviled ham, canned, 1 tablespoon	45
Frankfurter, 2 ounces	170
Pork link, 3" × 1/2"	125
Poultry, 3 ounces cooked:	
Chicken:	
Breast, fried, with bone	140
Drumstick, fried, with bone	130
Roasted, no skin	145
Duck, roasted, no skin	265
Goose, roasted, no skin	275
Turkey, roasted, no skin	165
Seafood, 3 ounces:	
Clams, canned	85
Cod, broiled	145
Crabmeat, canned	85
Fish sticks	150
Halibut, broiled	145
Lobster, canned	80
Oysters, raw	60
Salmon, pink, canned	120
Sardines, canned in oil	175
Scallops, steamed	95
Shrimp:	
Canned	100
French fried	190
Tuna, canned in oil	170

	Calories
Nuts	
Almonds, 1/4 cup	215
Brazil, 4	95
Cashews, 1/4 cup	195
Coconut, shredded, firmly packed, 1/2 cup	225
Hazelnut, 6	50
Peanuts, 1/4 cup	210
Pecans, 1/4 cup	185
Walnuts, 1/4 cup	200
Sauces *(2 tablespoons)*	
Butterscotch	205
Cheese	65
Chili	35
Chocolate	85
Fudge	125
Hollandaise	95
Lemon	65
Tartar	150
Tomato	40
White	50
Worcestershire	25
Soups *(made with water, 1 cup)*	
Bean with pork	170
Beef Noodle	70
Bouillon	30
Clam chowder	80
Cream of chicken	95
Cream of mushroom	135
Oyster stew	120
Split pea	145
Tomato	90
Vegetable beef	80
Sweets	
Candies:	
Caramels, 1 medium	40
Chocolate:	
Bar, plain, 1 ounce	150
Bar, with almonds, 1 ounce	140
Kisses, 7	150

	Calories
Fudge, 1″ square	105
Gum drops, 1 large, or 8 small	35
Jelly beans, 10	65
Lollipop, 2¼″ diameter	110
Marshmallow, 1 large	25
Peanut brittle, 2½″ square	110
Jams and preserves, 1 tablespoon	55
Jellies, 1 tablespoon	50
Doughnuts:	
Cake type	125
Cake type, sugared	150
Raised	125
Raised, jelly center	225
Eclair, custard filling, chocolate icing	315
Gelatin, fruit flavored, ½ cup	70
Gingerbread, 2″ square	205
Ice cream, ½ cup	130
Ice milk, ½ cup:	
Hardened	100
Soft-serve	135
Pies, 9″ diameter, ¹/₇:	
Apple	350
Blueberry	330
Cherry	350
Coconut custard	315
Custard	285
Lemon meringue	305
Mince	365
Peach	360
Pecan	490
Pumpkin	275
Raisin	280
Rhubarb	350
Pudding, ½ cup:	
Bread with raisins	210
Chocolate	195
Rice with raisins	140
Tapioca	110
Vanilla	140
Sherbet, ½ cup	130
Shortcake, strawberry	380

	Calories
Sugars, ½ cup:	
Brown	410
Granulated	385
Powdered	230
Syrups, 1 tablespoon:	
Chocolate-flavored	50
Corn	60
Honey	65
Maple	50
Molasses	50

Eggs

Boiled	80
Fried	110
Scrambled	110

Fats and Oils *(1 tablespoon)*

Butter	100
Cream:	
Coffee	30
Half and Half	20
Sour	25
Whipping	55
Lard	115
Margarine	100
Oil	125
Salad Dressings:	
Blue cheese	75
French	65
Mayonnaise	100
Mayonnaise type	65
Thousand Island	80

Fruits

Apple, 2½″ diameter	70
Apple juice, ½ cup	60
Applesauce, ½ cup:	
Canned, sweetened	115
Canned, unsweetened	50
Apricot:	
Canned, sweetened, ½ cup	110

	Calories
Canned, unsweetened, ½ cup	40
Fresh, 3 medium	55
Stewed, unsweetened, ½ cup	120
Avocado, 3½″ × 4″, ½	165
Banana, 6″	80
Blackberries, fresh, ½ cup	40
Blueberries, fresh, ½ cup	40
Cantaloupe, 5″ diameter, ½	60
Cherry:	
Canned, sweetened, ½ cup	90
Canned, unsweetened, ½ cup	50
Fresh, ½ cup	60
Maraschino, 1 large	10
Cranberry sauce, sweetened, ½ cup	200
Dates, 3 medium	80
Fig, dried, 1 large	60
Fruit cocktail, sweetened, ½ cup	75
Grapes, green seedless, ½ cup	50
Grape juice, canned, ½ cup	80
Grapefruit, ½ medium	50
Grapefruit juice, canned, ½ cup	50
Honeydew melon, 5″ diameter, ¼	35
Lemon juice, 3 tablespoons	15
Nectarine	30
Orange, 2⅝″ diameter	65
Orange juice, unsweetened, ½ cup	60
Peach:	
Canned, sweetened, ½ cup	100
Canned, unsweetened, ½ cup	40
Fresh, 2″ diameter	35
Pear:	
Canned, sweetened, ½ cup	100
Canned, unsweetened, ½ cup	40
Fresh, 3″ × 2½″	100
Pineapple:	
Canned, sweetened, 1 large slice	90
Fresh, ½ cup	40
Pineapple juice, unsweetened, ½ cup	70
Plum:	
Fresh, 2″ diameter	25
Italian prune, canned, sweetened, 3 medium	100

	Calories
Prunes, 4 medium	70
Prune juice, ½ cup	100
Pumpkin, canned, ½ cup	40
Raisins, dry, 2 tablespoons	60
Raspberries, fresh, ½ cup	35
Rhubarb, stewed, sweetened, ½ cup	190
Strawberries, ½ cup:	
Fresh	30
Frozen, sweetened	140
Tangerine, 2½″ diameter	40
Watermelon, 4″ × 8″ wedge	115

Vegetables

Asparagus, cooked, ½ cup	20
Bamboo shoots, ½ cup	20
Beans, ½ cup:	
Baked, no pork	150
Green, cooked	15
Kidney, cooked	115
Lima, cooked	95
Beets, cooked, ½ cup	25
Beet greens, cooked, ½ cup	20
Broccoli, cooked, ½ cup	20
Brussels sprouts, cooked, ½ cup	30
Cabbage, ½ cup:	
Cooked	15
Raw	10
Carrot, raw or cooked, ½ cup or 1 (5½″ × 1″)	25
Cauliflower, cooked, ½ cup	15
Celery, 8″ × ½″ stalk	5
Corn:	
Canned, whole kernel, ½ cup	85
Cob, 5″ × 1¾″ ear	70
Cucumber, 12 slices	10
Eggplant, raw, 2 slices	25
Kale, cooked, ½ cup	15
Lettuce, Iceberg, 4¾″ diameter, ¼	15
Mushrooms, canned, ¼ cup	10
Okra, cooked, 3″ × ⅝″, 8 pods	25

Calories

Onion:
   Cooked, 1/2 cup — 30
   Green, 6 small — 20
Parsnip, cooked, 1/2 cup — 50
Peas, cooked, 1/2 cup — 60
Pepper, raw, 1 medium — 15
Potato:
   Cooked, 2 1/4″ diameter — 80
   French fried, 2″ × 1/2″, 10 pieces — 155
   Mashed with milk, 1/2 cup — 65
   Sweet, 1/2 cup — 120
Radishes, 4 small — 5
Rutabaga, cooked, 1/2 cup — 35
Sauerkraut, 1/2 cup — 20
Spinach, cooked, 1/2 cup — 20
Squash, cooked, 1/2 cup:
   Summer — 15
   Winter — 65
Tomato:
   Canned, 1/2 cup — 25
   Fresh, 3″ diameter — 40
Tomato juice, 1/2 cup — 20
Turnip, cooked, 1/2 cup — 20
Water chestnuts, 4 — 20

Miscellaneous
Catsup, 1 tablespoon — 15
Cocoa, 1 tablespoon — 20
Chocolate, bitter, 1 ounce — 145
Gelatin, unflavored, 1 envelope — 25
Gravy, 1 tablespoon — 40
Herring, pickled, 1″ × 1/2″ — 50
Ice cream bar, chocolate covered — 145
Mustard, prepared, 1 teaspoon — 5
Olives:
   Green, 4 medium — 15
   Ripe, 3 small — 15
Peanut butter, 1 tablespoon — 95

Pickles:	
Dill, 3¾″ × 1¼″	10
Relish, 1 tablespoon	20
Sweet, 2½″ × ¾″	20
Pizza, cheese, 14″ diameter, 1/8	185
Popcorn, oil added, 1 cup	40
Popsicle	70
Potato chips, 10	115
Pretzels, 3⅛″, 5 sticks	10
Vinegar, 2 tablespoons	5
Yeast, dry, active, 1 package	20
Yogurt, 1 cup:	
Made from skimmed milk	125
Made from whole milk	150

Index